Abuse
Domestic Violence, Workplace and School Bullying

Abuse

Domestic Violence, Workplace and School Bullying

JIM O'SHEA

ATRIUM

First published in 2011 by Atrium
Atrim is an imprint of Cork University Press,
Youngline Industrial Estate,
Pouladuff Road, Togher,
Cork, Ireland

British Library Cataloguing in Publication Data

A CIP catalogue record for this book is available from the British Library.

ISBN: 978-1-85594-217-2

Typeset by Tower Books, Ballincollig, Co. Cork
Printed by Gutenberg Press, Malta

www.corkuniversitypress.com

Contents

Acknowledgements

Some time ago, I wrote a series of articles on abuse for a local magazine, *The Tipp Tatler*. Many people found these helpful, and suggested that I write a book on abuse. I decided to do so, and as I delved deeper, I began to realise how complex this behaviour is. I wondered if it was possible to explore it sufficiently is such a small book. I hope I have succeeded in doing so, and it was only possible because of the feedback from a number of people. I want to thank my friend, Dr Donal O'Callaghan, for his many insightful comments and exacting criticism that has helped me shape the book, and clarify many aspects of abuse. Despite being extremely busy in her teaching work in the US, my eldest daughter, Frances, gave me much moral and practical support. She patiently read many of the chapters, and stringently applied the scalpel, so that the contents became clearer. I am extremely grateful to 'Linda', who told her story and made the book more human and more interesting. I am also thankful to 'Anna' for allowing me in include her 'unsent letter' to her workplace abuser, and I wish to thank 'Alex' for sharing his story of enmeshment with me. I am very grateful to Mrs Mary Rita Korzan for allowing me to quote her lovely poem, *When You Thought I Wasn't Looking*. I want to acknowledge my wife, Mary, who does not complain when I closet myself away for months to write books. I want, also, to thank the many people from various organisations who gave me valuable information, and clarified issues for me. I also want to express my gratitude to Maria O'Donovan, Mike Collins and other staff of Cork University Press (Atrium) for their kindness and courtesy Their professionalism and attention to detail inspired me. Finally, it would be remiss of me not to thank, on behalf of all victims, those authors named in the bibliography whose expertise as therapists, researchers and writers has helped to relieve the distress of so many people.

Introduction

They stumble in mind-darkness,
Joyless in their souls' destruction.
Shame cloaked.
Forgetting who they were,
Not knowing who they are.
Dehumanised in their wound-filled souls,
Tears unnoticed,
Hearts' hidden hurts.
Afraid,
They stumble on,
Awaiting redemption
Courage
To confront the destroyer.
And live again.

Jim O'Shea

The majority of relationships are healthy, and abuse can never thrive in a healthy relationship. Love is the basis of all healthy relationships. When I was a child, I learned that we should love our fellow humans irrespective of creed, class or colour. I learned that love was patient, kind and tolerant. Behaviours within an intimate relationship should demonstrate love, patience and parity, where we can peacefully sort out our difficulties. The relationship must be nurtured with patience and generosity, and as much unconditional love as possible. Our needs must be substantially met, so that we can feel our power, experience intimacy, feel that we are loved, have fun, and have the freedom 'to be'. The healthy relationship encourages disclosure without fear of nasty repercussions, breeds trust, and allows scope for mutual and individual space.

Unfortunately, however, this is not always the case and abuse is common and universal. It is perpetrated by both men and women. It is found in every social, cultural, economic and racial background. Professionals, white-collar workers, religious leaders, well-educated people are just as likely to be abusive as any other. Throughout the book I will give you a few statistics merely to show how extensive it is globally. These statistics are shocking, and mainly refer to developed countries. I shudder at what may be happening in developing countries such as Uganda, where women are poor, deprived and do most of the farm work. They risk being assaulted, raped, and having their children abducted.

Governments all over the world are now exercised about the reality of abuse. I would like to pay tribute to the Irish government for setting out a national strategy on domestic, sexual and gender-based violence for the period 2010–2014. This is explained in detail by a report compiled by Cosc, The National Office for the Prevention of Domestic, Sexual and Gender-Based Violence. Cosc (an Irish word meaning 'to stop' or 'to prevent') was established in 2007 with the key responsibility to ensure the delivery of a co-ordinated response to sexual and gender-based violence. It is concerned with domestic and sexual violence against women and men. It is an executive office of the Department of Justice and Law Reform, but works on a cross-government perspective, covering co-ordination across justice, health, housing, education, family support, and non-government organisations. Its purpose is to ensure the delivery of an effective service through these departments and organisations.

You can learn more about Cosc and its specific tasks from its website, and I would strongly recommend that Irish readers of this book should have a look at the report referred to above. The organisation's strategy vision is shown in it, and among other aspects, emphasises that by 2014 there should be a broader understanding of domestic, sexual and gender-based violence, and the existence in Ireland of 'greater confidence in high quality and consistent services'. Hopefully, this will happen, even within the context of a severe economic downturn and a series of harsh budgets.

This book examines five types of abuse – physical, emotional/psychological/mental, verbal, sexual, and financial/economic. Generally, they will be explored in the context of intimate relationships. Bullying in the workplace, which can contain all of these types of abuse, is also explored. The book will focus on adult victims and highlight the harrowing behaviours of abusers. However, because of its importance, I have also included a chapter on child abuse.

People need to know what boundaries are before they can understand abuse. This is explored in the opening chapter, and will enlighten parents on child formation. Parents will also learn about dysfunctional child development in chapter 2, which looks at the creation of the abusive personality.

The report by Cosc shows that the Irish population has a high level of awareness of the reality of domestic abuse, yet my experience is that many people do not realise that they are victims. People reared in abusive homes see it as normal, and others from warm, caring homes are ignorant of what it means, and may spend years in abusive relationships, struggling to understand why the person they love is trying to harm them. Many victims are highly educated, and still they do not see the underlying pattern of control or realise that the abusive behaviour is planned and deliberate. This is well illustrated in some of the stories in Elaine Weiss's book *Surviving Domestic Violence. Voices of Women Who Broke Free.* One of my clients, 'Linda', tells her harrowing story, and brings us into a marriage where her husband displays all the characteristics of the abuser.

Thankfully, victims such as Linda can break free and live independent and happy lives; and the book looks at leaving, surviving and recovering from an abusive relationship. I hope, also, that those with abusive tendencies will read it, stop and think, and realise just how damaging their behaviour is. The final chapter offers suggestions on how to expel this destructive menace from their lives.

Abuse is not about alcohol addiction. Some abusers may be alcoholics, but abuse does not stem from that. Someone who is not abusive will not be abusive when either drunk or sober, and someone who is abusive will be abusive, drunk or sober. One of Elaine Weiss's narrators puts this well when she says that her partner hit her when he was sober, but he hit her harder when he was drunk. Sometimes abusers will use alcohol as an excuse to carry out abusive acts and to punish the victim, and then pretend that they do not remember what they did when they were drunk. Victims may be confused because abuse shares some of the features of addiction insofar as both can escalate, both may involve minimising, manipulation, blaming, and so on.

Abuse is driven by toxic shame and rage, and, I believe, is engraved in the biology of the brain. It is also the offspring of childhood conditioning and can be a learned behaviour, underpinned by irrational thoughts, beliefs and values. Driven by these, abusers use power and control to humiliate the victims, trample on their boundaries, and exert control over them.

Among other aspects, this book will explore how the abuser tries to control the victim's time and their material resources; controlling by body language and gestures, by confusing the victim and defining their reality, by blaming, and by reducing the victim's status through demeaning behaviours, violence, sexual control, or perhaps financial manipulation.

A book of this size cannot explore every aspect of abuse, but I feel confident that it will be sufficient to educate you on the causes, nature and consequences of this behaviour. It is designed to help you. It has no other purpose.

Chapter 1

Boundaries

Foetus-like in shell unbreached
The wounded child lies
Alone
Within the adult.
Filled with pain.
Confused,
Not knowing why.
A frozen wasteland,
Where there is no warmth,
Where intimacy burns the soul,
And leaves the spirit
Mourning the loss of love
Yearning for the joy of soul-togetherness.
Never.

Jim O'Shea

I believe that understanding boundaries is one of the major defences against abuse, and is of paramount importance when attempting to recover from its aftermath. The concept of boundaries is not easily understood, so I will allow my close friend, Alex, to share his story with you as an introduction to the reality of boundaries.

> For about 40 years, I struggled with intense feelings of shame, anger, and feeling that I was not a good enough human being. I had no idea why I felt like this, and I didn't know who I was. My judgement was always poor, and I worried about offending others. I made every effort to be nice to everyone and to please everyone, and I kept

5

up a facade of being happy. I eventually admitted to myself that I hated my mother, and opened up a can of worms that I had kept closed all my life. My mother, not deliberately, tried to keep me for herself. She did not allow me to emotionally separate from her, and I became an angry rebel. When the time came, I couldn't wait to get away from home. I was ok until about the age of 13. I adored my mother, but at around that age I began to hate her. I never admitted it, and thought it was sinful, so I began to hate myself for feeling this way. How could I hate my mother who gave me so many material things! Somehow, I felt part of her. I felt smothered, and did not feel whole or separate. It was a horrible feeling of unease and pain. Worst of all I had no feeling for anyone. I never felt any remorse, and this lack of sympathy tormented me. I knew it was wrong. But where did it come from, I often asked myself. The more ruthless I grew the more I hated myself. Looking back, the most obvious sign that I was meeting my mother's needs was the fact that I was over 7 years of age before she sent me to school. Most children in those days went to school at 4 or 5 years old. This entanglement messed up my life for a long time, and affected all those close to me.

Abusive behaviour humiliates the victim, and refuses to recognise the dignity of the human being. It is a contemptuous exertion of power over another. When people suffer severe abuse their emotional boundaries not only become blurred, but they often lose any sense of them.

So what are boundaries? It may be helpful to think of our skin as our most basic boundary. It protects us, keeps us together, allows us to nourish ourselves with food and remain healthy, and protects us from germs and disease. Think of how we nourish it, protecting it from the sun, pampering it with expensive creams and lotions, binding its wounds. Worth taking care of! We know what it is like when somebody gets under our skin! How irritating it is!

Boundaries are our personal space in our relationships.

They show where personal responsibility begins and ends. They define the limits we set. They are the physical, emotional, mental, sexual, spiritual, financial and relational space that we need to exist as independent human beings. Within this space, we are responsible for our thoughts, feelings, values, behaviours, choices, dreams, gifts, desires, needs, beliefs and limits. Naturally, it is important that we, rather than others, control these. Our boundaries give us the authority and the power to be assertive. To say 'no'. They are there to keep in the good and keep out the bad. Boundaries are the haven where we nourish our souls. The cradles of self-care.

They define our separate identity. By honouring them, we communicate our sense of self-respect. They help us discover who we are. Any counsellor will tell you that they have clients who say that they have no sense of self. They do not know who they are. Our boundaries are the emotional and psychological indications that we are separate from other people; that we are not enmeshed. Enmeshment may seem like intimacy, but it is a dangerous merging of ourselves with another, whereby our individuality and identity is lost. Our personal power and control cannot exist in this type of relationship. Our independence is eroded, our sense of self weakened, so that we are filled with confusion about our identity. It means that I do not know where I end and you begin, because my boundaries are fused with someone else's.

Sometimes enmeshment can mean that a child, as in the case of Alex, is forced to meet the needs of a parent, and this type of role reversal eventually makes the child feel inadequate, because children cannot properly fulfil the role of an adult. They are not permitted to be children, their emotional needs are not being met, and so they may harbour feelings of abandonment. They bring this to adulthood. It can also mean that the self-system of the child was never allowed to develop normally, so that he becomes an emotional slave to meet the narcissistic needs of the parent. This emotional neglect sows the seeds of fear, low self-esteem, shame and anger, which one day will emerge as a poisonous bloom. This adult may then exhibit extreme selfishness, lack of empathy, a tendency to control, being negative, using others, aggression, and a whole host of other undesirable characteristics and behaviours, including codependent behaviours.

People living in codependency (e.g. an alcoholic whose spouse colludes in allowing him/her to evade their responsibility) have weak boundaries. Codependency is born in childhood when a child is unable to build safe boundaries, and absorbs the negative feelings of its parents. In adulthood, the true self (the newborn infant) is lost. In this particular type of enmeshment the child, who struggled so valiantly and so vainly to fulfil a parent's needs, now, as an adult, equally vainly tries to fulfil the needs of an addicted (or abusive) partner. Codependency is a painful, debilitating and restricting condition, and is often part of an abusive relationship. Part of healing is for the victim to step back, create a boundary and become aware that he or she did not cause, cannot control and cannot cure the addiction of the other person.

A codependent relationship is an unhealthy one, so when the boundary is created the codependent person can become real, and reach happiness and peace. Therefore, healthy boundaries are essential if we wish to foster a healthy relationship. When they are inappropriately breached, we feel a sense of outrage, hurt and, in the case of violence, a sense of helplessness. Healthy boundaries enable us to develop relationships based on trust, stability and respect, and tell others how we expect to be treated. They create a sense of safety in a relationship, and are a comfort zone. They allow for and respect each person's values, beliefs, thoughts and emotions. Healthy boundaries are elastic, expanding to keep some at a distance and contracting to allow others intimacy. The scope of boundaries, therefore, depends on the nature of a relationship. The boundaries of a married couple differ from those of a parent and child, and the boundaries of friends differ from the boundaries between work colleagues. What is appropriate in one case is inappropriate in another. For example, there are boundaries between a counsellor and a client; if the counsellor steps outside these boundaries, he or she may be abusing the client.

Some people's boundaries are so rigid that they are unable to have any real emotional relationship. They dissociate (make themselves emotionally distant), and refuse to let anyone in, or if they do, they quickly cast them out as the discomfort caused by intimacy is too great. This becomes a never-ending spiral of acceptance and rejection, creating confusion and hurt in the other person. They erect their rigid boundaries to protect some hurt, probably from childhood. It is extraordinary how a child abused at a very young age can create the most rigid boundaries; an impenetrable shell to protect itself. This arrest of emotional development may come from traumatic events such as rejection, emotional abandonment, sexual abuse, emotional abuse, and physical abuse. That shell does not weaken as they grow into adults when it continues to protect that open wound inflicted on their psyche so long ago. It is a sad reality that boundaries have to be rigid and impenetrable in such cases. The child must protect that painful wound. However, protecting the wound, although vital, has disastrous consequences. The victim shuts himself off from human warmth and all parties in the relationship suffer. There is a possibility that that child may become an adult abuser, because he cannot relate emotionally to another human.

Other people have gapped boundaries and rightly erect them on some occasions, but fail on others. They create uncertainty and conflict in their intimate relationships. Partners never know what to expect. There are also people who have no boundaries, and allow others to invade their space and vice versa. These people do not know what boundaries are, because they never had the opportunity to construct them.

People with gapped or no boundaries are able to relate better than those in the impenetrable shell, but they find it difficult to have stable relationships, and may indulge in behaviours which create many other difficulties for them. They may smother those with whom they relate. They may try to be more than human, and always strive to be nice to others, trying to 'fix' them, giving unwanted advice, taking on the feelings of others, taking over from them and thus making them powerless. Their focus is on the problems of others rather than on themselves. In doing this they step inside the boundaries of others, become over friendly, confide personal information and cause embarrassment.

People with weak boundaries find it very difficult to say no, and so collude with abuse. They may be unable to say no because of unhealthy core instincts, and, like Alex, may dislike hurting other people's feelings; they may have a fear of abandonment, or an inclination to be dependent on others. They may also have a fear of being shamed, or of being seen as selfish or being overly strict. In other words, they live in a world of uncertainty, sometimes fearing the anger and retribution of another, wallow in low self-esteem and confusion, and drown in their shame, guilt, anger and exhaustion. They allow the abuser an easy entrance to their personal space to exert control over them. The well-known American psychotherapist Charles Whitfield has an extensive checklist on boundaries in chapter 2 of his book *Boundaries and Relationships*.

Our relationships can also founder on the jagged rocks of self-boundary deficiencies, where we struggle in chaos and shifting sands. Self-boundaries are the limits we set for ourselves, as against the limits we set on others. They are our internal boundary struggles. These may be concretised as food addictions, problems with money such as overspending, inability to budget, borrowing and difficulties with credit, to name but a few. Self-boundary problems are also likely to arise in the context of time boundaries. People with weak self-boundaries find timekeeping difficult. They create tensions and misery for others by being late for meetings and appointments. They also find it difficult to complete deadlines and tasks. Failure to complete tasks may stem from core shame, the great destroyer of boundaries. Such people lack good judgement, may fear being successful, are easily distracted, and unable to focus on the task to be completed. They create the conditions where either abusiveness or victimhood can flourish.

Those with weak boundaries often conceal their real feelings, and even if they strongly disagree with something, they pretend to agree. This leaves them open to becoming victims of abuse, and ultimately to feel the bitter taste of powerlessness, and to flounder in a state of confusion. They become fearful of being involved in enjoyable activities and take part in activities that they do not like. They blunder along, ignoring their needs, not taking care of themselves psychologically, mentally, spiritually or physically. They take on the feelings of others as their spongy boundaries fail to protect them, but absorb the pain of others. Sometimes people with weak boundaries retreat from social intercourse and ruminate in their loneliness, unable to share their vulnerable selves. Their inner child remains alone and unnourished. If you wish to know more about the inner child, you might like to read Luccia Capacchione's book *Recovery of Your Inner Child*.

If we have healthy boundaries we will know if they have been breached by the discomfort we feel when this happens. We may also feel discomfort if we breach the boundaries of others. Thus, good boundaries not only protect us from non-violent abuse, but also alert us if we are abusing others. When our boundaries are properly formed, our judgement is good. We do not, for example, see the feelings of others as our responsibility. We are responsible only for our own feelings. Thus having good boundaries enables us to take care of ourselves. Only each individual knows what is good for him or her. Knowing our needs is part of the space within our boundaries. Having good boundaries also helps us not to be people pleasers, stops us from feeling guilty if we disappoint others, or from trying to protect others.

Boundaries help us to fight against irrational thoughts. It is our job to care about others, but not to take care of them. Taking care of them prevents them making choices. We may not agree with the choices of others. Of course, we are entitled to state our opinion about the choices, but ultimately we must respect them. Healthy boundaries have fundamental characteristics. We are aware of them, they protect the real us, they are clear; they are as firm as we wish them to be, they are flexible, and we know when and how to maintain them.

Where then do we build healthy boundaries? Who teaches us to build them? Ideally, parents are the main teachers. They demonstrate healthy boundaries by their own behaviour within and without the home. Children also learn boundaries when they have a secure attachment to their parents, especially to the main caregiver. A secure attachment means that they feel safe in the warm love of their caregiver, but are gradually allowed to detach and extend their relationship to others, and finally to separate fully from their parents. As Donald Dutton, Professor of Psychology at the University of British Columbia, points out, the important element of secure attachment is attunement whereby the mother's response matches the emotional state shown by the infant. She does this through sounds, facial expression, and gestures. The Irish writer Liam Ó Flaithearta, in his book *Dúil*, has a marvellous story about a baby which illustrates this very well. This simple story tells about a small child gradually separating from his mother, and the excitement that he feels as he explores his environment, yet at the same time keeping a watchful eye on her. The story ends with the child snuggled in his mother's lap dreaming about further exploration until he will eventually take his place in the wide world. Unwittingly, Ó Flaithearta probably penned the first illustration of a secure attachment by a child to his mother!

However, to understand abuse we also need to understand what an insecure attachment means. For our purposes, an insecure attachment can mean a fearful or dismissive attachment. A child who has a dismissive attachment appears to be independent of mother, can crawl away from her and return without paying any attention to her, almost avoiding her. Separation does not seem to bother this child. On the other hand, a child with a fearful attachment becomes terrified at leaving mother, and clings to her with all his might. I believe that fearful attach-ment, in particular, can breed the hidden raging serpent of abuse that will someday strike and wound. Fortunately, this happens only in a small minority of such cases.

The American psychologists Henry Cloud and John Townsend give a good explanation of boundaries from birth to late teens, by which time boundaries should be well estab-lished. From birth to five months, the child feels at one with the primary caregiver, although somewhere in that period it begins to sense that it is a separate entity. From five to ten months the child begins to separate, while retaining the parents as an anchor and sensing the limits being set. By three years, the child begins to understand limits, responsibilities and consequences for its behaviour. It still, however, clings to attachment with parents in its increasing independence. During the three to five year period parents have much bound-ary work to do, as sex-role development occurs in the child. This is where enmeshment by needy parents, such as Alex's mother, can undermine boundary building. It is vital that parents keep the boundary between child and parent clear.

The period of 6 to 11 prepares the child for adolescence. Children continue to learn how they are similar to, yet different from, others. The self (their unique identity) is further explored and social roles developed more. Children learn the bound-aries inherent in connecting with same-sex peers, and of finishing tasks through schoolwork and all that involves.

Adolescence brings with it sexual maturation, identity formation, and relationships with the opposite sex. Significant separation takes place as a preparation for adulthood. This can be sad and difficult for parents, but it is an important time in the building of boundaries, when feelings, beliefs, behaviours and values are being mulled over by the adolescent within their boundaries. During this stage it is important for parents to continue to model and show healthy boundaries to enable the adolescent to achieve a healthy sense of self. Their role is more influencing rather than controlling. They loosen the rein to allow a healthy development of the adolescent's boundaries. This freedom enables the adolescent to relate healthily to others.

Apart from secure attachment and modelling, parents also teach boundaries in practical ways. A few of the things they can do is to help their children identify trustworthy peers and teach them to say 'no' to peer pressure. They make them aware of the importance of avoiding those who might harm them in any way, and teach them to respect the physical space of others. Parents could also explain to their children that sharing private thoughts and personal information with strangers is not safe. Parents teach responsibility, set limits and teach the child (who wants instant gratification) patience.

I grew up in an era when the motto that 'children should be seen and not heard' was frequently voiced! Parents of that era did the best they could, but, in a sense, that dictum diluted children's boundaries, and made them vulnerable to abuse when they reached adulthood. They were in effect muzzled, silenced and shamed, and this is what happens in an abusive relationship. Therefore, it is important for parents to allow and encourage their children to express their feelings, especially anger. In my childhood, showing anger to parents was frowned on. It was seen as wrong and even sinful. Anger was one of the 'seven deadly sins' noted in the catechism! Encouraging children to ask questions and be inquisitive also fosters healthy boundary development.

We have already seen the psychological consequences of the enmeshment and codependency that stem from poor boundary development. However, we also now know that separation difficulties can result in permanent changes in brain chemistry. Shame, rage and dysfunctional feelings are physically embossed or burnt into the brain, and, as will be shown, it can take a long time to erase that neural wound.

Children of dysfunctional families are unlikely to have proper boundaries, and when they grow to adulthood, they

will find it very difficult to help their own children build good boundaries. Therefore, inability to build proper boundaries stretches across generations, and may be related to abuse, which may also be trans-generational. Parents who have been toxically shamed are unable to teach their children boundaries. They do the opposite. The pain and needs of dysfunctional parents are so great that the needs of the children for safety, security, respect and comfort are relegated, and as they grow up, they are unable to form a healthy sense of their own identities, and hence do not understand what boundaries are. It is likely that their boundaries will be unstable and cause them to swing between engulfment on the one hand and abandonment on the other, leading to dysfunctional relationships as adults.

In the main, parents do not deliberately set out to harm their child. However, if they operate in a dysfunctional way the child internalises (takes in) their negative feelings about themselves, and models himself upon their dysfunction, thus laying part of the foundation of the abusive personality, discussed in another chapter. This is catastrophic. The unfortunate child will only have a distorted image of the real or true self, and this distortion remains in adult life. The distortion is reinforced if the ugly reality of abuse enters the life of the person, and will be looked at again in the chapter on child abuse.

The concept of the real self is very emotional for me, and once drew my tears as I read one of Carl Rogers' books in the foyer of the Ardilaun House Hotel in Galway. I was then in my fifties, and I can only agree with Charles Whitfield that those of us with blurred boundaries and a false self stumble through life and only discover how to recover after mid-life. So much can be wasted when boundaries are imperfect. Clearly, if we have not adequate boundaries it is important for our happiness and our independence to build some, and protect ourselves from abuse. It is our right, duty and responsibility to protect ourselves.

How, therefore, do we go about building proper boundaries in adulthood? First, we must educate ourselves and understand what they are. It can be a moving experience to begin the construction of boundaries because it involves a quest for our real selves. The real self is utterly lovable, because it is the self that entered this world as a tiny infant. I believe that we can only build good boundaries as adults if we love ourselves, but we must first find that self. Then we will automatically erect proper boundaries to protect that person we love. Loving ourselves means loving all of ourselves, the negative as well as the positive traits that we all have. If there is any part of ourselves that we do not love, then we do not love ourselves, and become split within ourselves.

Loving ourselves, of course, means having the inestimable gift of good self-esteem (esteem for the self), which is our best defence against abuse. This strong sense of self-worth and self-value must lie within ourselves. Outside factors such as work or achievements is not a foundation for true self-esteem. Clearly if our boundaries are imperfect, we do not have much self-esteem because the self is lost or hidden. Building self-esteem normally comes from our parents giving us as much unconditional love as possible. If this does not happen, we must find someone to help us explore our lives, and in a mysterious way arrive at self-esteem. This is what happens in the safety of a counselling room where we retrace our life journey with a non-judgemental stranger, who helps us to emotionally re-experience the negative experiences of the past, and especially of childhood. The important thing here is that we are taking control; we make the decision to go to a counsellor, a self-help group or any safe supportive person.

In my own counselling practice, I have seen people with damaged self-esteem become confident, assertive individuals as they again felt past pain and confronted the negative thoughts that they had imbibed as children. As counselling progressed, they automatically became enabled to set clear boundaries. That is real happiness, and it is well earned. People who have been shamed are likely to be addicted, perhaps to alcohol, work, sex, or whatever. It may take years to work through the addiction and to recover. Then the time comes to handle the inner core of toxic shame, fear and anger, so that eventually self-love comes.

As self-esteem grows and we clarify our boundaries, we will be in a position to defend them in a healthy way. And what do we do when there is an emotional, sexual or physical attack made on them? We move away, we express our displeasure; we let it be known that this is our space. It is about being aware of how we feel. It is acknowledging our feelings to ourselves and letting others know too. It is always good to begin our sentence with the words 'I feel'. It is about communication, the basis of a healthy relationship. Without it, there is always the danger of abuse. Silence is one of the principal ways of allowing the poisonous weed of abuse to flourish.

Communication means speaking in a non-judgemental way, specifically naming the behaviour that causes us displeasure, saying 'I feel angry/fearful when you shout at me', 'I don't like it when you touch me like that', and so on. Communication is also about making the consequences clear if the other person continues to treat us in an unacceptable way. It involves making choices about staying in an abusive environment or leaving, because even if we have good boundaries they can be breached by violence, whether we like it or not. A sense of love of self, good self-esteem and boundaries make it easier to make the often difficult decision to leave the person we love. Our boundaries empower us; they enable us to make and to own our decisions, and stop us being victims.

We need others to sow this self-esteem, and we need others to help us build our boundaries. I do not believe that we can do it on our own. These others must be safe, skilled, caring people, who are not trying to fix us, but support us in acting responsibly. Being safe means that they listen and hear us, accept us, support us, do not judge us, that they are clear and direct, have clear boundaries and are real in how they relate to us. Of course, it takes humility for us to expose ourselves to another, but humility is part of healthy boundaries, it allows us to experience emotional nourishment from others.

Chapter 2

The Abusive Personality:
warning signs of possible abuse in new and existing relationships

I grew close to you,
And felt the caress of your love
Enfolding me in its warm embrace.
The wound in my soul soothed
By the gentleness of your voice.
I did not feel the chill that sometimes came
And went as quickly.
And then persisted
And grew colder,
Until I bathed in the coldness of disdain,
And felt the reins of anger haul me in
And shackle me in chains of scorn
And mockery.
And then my spirit
Hung its head in shame.
And confused spirit
Smiled
When flattery returned.
Groaned
When icy chill blew its cold face
Across my soul.
Again
Again
And again.

Jim O'Shea

Although good boundaries are your best defence against abuse, you need further tools to protect yourself. One of these is aware-ness at the beginning of a relationship of the warning signs that a partner may be potentially abusive. These signs and behaviours will be mentioned again throughout the chapters dealing with the various types of abuse.

Early detection will help to prevent you falling into a fully-fledged abusive relationship. This is all the more important if your boundaries are unstable. Few relationships begin in an abusive way. You may find your partner charming, charismatic, attentive, loving, romantic, polite, amusing, helpful and handsome. Equally desirable, he may share many of your interests. You may think that you have a real soul mate. He may be a prominent member of the community, a politician, a lawyer, an architect, a doctor, a professor, and so on.

If your self-esteem is low, if you have brought feelings of abandonment from childhood, and if you feel not good enough, that person's initial attention will make you feel wanted, flattered and fortunate. It is easy to be disarmed in those early stages by charm. Abusers often try to form an intimate relationship very quickly, claiming love at first sight, and will try to pressurise the would-be victim to commit at an early stage. Linda's husband, the 'charming' Stephen, displays this characteristic shortly after meeting her.

> Within a few weeks, he had told me he loved me. And to be honest it was so intense between us that it didn't come as a real shock . . . A couple of weeks before Christmas 2005 I came home from work one evening, and called for Stephen to do the shopping like we generally would do – he said he was nearly ready and to come into the kitchen for a minute. I went in and he led me to the sitting room, where candles were lighting and two glasses of wine were poured out. That evening he asked me to marry him. I knew it was quick, but I was so happy and everything seemed to be perfect, and I said yes.
>
> I always remember something he said to me that evening after I said yes – he said that if I had said 'no' or needed time to think about it – that he would have left and it would have been over. I found that harsh, but at

the same time, I was glad that I didn't say no, if that was the case. I loved this man, he was a good man, and they are hard to come by. So, in my happiness I paid little attention to his comments.

When you find that your charming suitor is looking for a quick commitment is the best time to use your intuition. Research has shown that a woman's intuition is the best predictor if a partner will be abusive to her. The charm, however, can disarm you, and make you go against your gut instinct.

Abusers cannot hide their tendencies for very long. The honeymoon period can be quite short, and will generally become evident shortly after marriage or commitment, when the process of enslavement begins, and the pedestal becomes a prison. The kind and attentive person will then show another face – an angry, and sometimes violent, face. This Jekyll and Hyde behaviour is one of the real warning signs of danger. Apparent love, affection and support are at some stage supplanted by the more dominant feelings of jealousy and envy. You may find yourself subjected to put downs and anger, rather than praise and nurturing. The pleasant Jekyll is kind and caring in public and the unpleasant Hyde is mean and nasty in private, leaving a legacy of confusion and bitterness in the victim's mind.

This Jekyll and Hyde split has something to do with an infant's needs not being met when he is dependent on his primary caregiver (usually the mother). A split occurs which is brought into adulthood. It could be a deeply rooted fear of abandonment, which is one of the most powerful negative experiences an infant can have. As it lurks in the adult, it creates a tormenting turmoil of boiling anger and fear. The Jekyll and Hyde personality also conceals the seeds of violence, which may manifest itself in sexual acting out or sexual tantrums. Sexual acting out and tantrums encompass a wide variety of behaviours. They are a withdrawal from intimate contact, and include sex addictions, risky sexual behaviour, and making sexual fantasies a reality.

The characteristics and behaviours of the Jekyll and Hyde personality are well illustrated by Stephen, who demanded an early commitment from Linda. He swept her off her feet with his charm, quickly married and then cruelly abandoned her. It is a shocking experience to be loved so warmly and then treated so cruelly. It is very difficult for the victim to take this in.

> I met my husband in 2005. I thought I had received all my lucky stars at once. Never had I felt so close to anyone, and felt such companionship. We were a couple, and more than that we were best friends as well, and really, to be honest, we were each other's life. We both had done everything together in every sense of the word. Rarely would you see one without the other. My husband when I met him was a caring, loving, respectful, good-looking man that I was mad about. I used to think to myself – I have met the one – how lucky I am. I have met a man that loves me and wants to spend every day with me.

The care and the love masked the control as Stephen took charge of the relationship, and how quickly it developed. Linda was unsuspecting as she allowed him to dictate.

> One night at his father's house, where he was staying at the time, he blurted out in front of his father that we were moving in together. This was all news to me. We had never discussed it. But at the time I was so happy and I wanted to be with him and he with me. I went along with it, and said, 'What's the point waiting if we are happy. We will be happy living together – we are together practically all the time anyway.'

The blissful experience continued with a 'beautiful wedding day' and a 'magical' honeymoon in Venice. Her delight was increased when she discovered that she had become pregnant on the honeymoon. Her dream had come true – 'to meet a lovely man that I could share my life with and be happily married and have a family'.

This dream was soon shattered, and Linda describes it as like a switch being flicked – and a different person appearing. The initial change in Stephen's behaviour quickly worsened. Linda was bewildered by it, because Stephen expressed delight and interest in her pregnancy, and promised that he would be very much involved when the child was born. The change began with a 'few words' over some trivial matter. Stephen left the house and did not return that night.

> At 11.30, he still wasn't home. This was the first time he had done this to me. I tried ringing his phone and he wouldn't answer. I sent a text to come home but then he turned off his phone. I was so upset I spent the night crying. I rang my best friend; she called and tried to calm me down. I cried myself to sleep that night. I was so hurt that he could do this. I was pregnant with his child and how could he not come home to me! He knew I would be upset. Did he not worry that I was pregnant and that stress for the baby was not good? I felt guilty that night for being so upset because I was worried about the baby. He came back the next day and was so sorry. He explained that he needed to take some time to himself and he went out with his friends. He promised it wouldn't happen ever again. But it did. And each time I was hurt, but he generally would come home the next day so I would try and stay calm and not get too upset. I was very much along in my pregnancy and I knew I couldn't keep getting so upset for my baby's sake.

Linda's pain intensified when their baby, Jack, was born, because not only did Stephen renege on his promises to be an involved father, but also he effectively abandoned his young wife and newborn baby, in favour of going out with his friends, and behaving irresponsibly.

> I used to say to him 'you take me so for granted, I would like some time during the week or weekends to go off with my friends or do something but you are never around for me to go anywhere, and you never ask me do

I need you to stay with Jack. You just presume all the time that I am doing nothing and will be at the house to mind Jack'. Then he started losing his jobs, or he would fall out with his employers. He moved from quite a few jobs so there was no sense of security. He gradually built up his days of disappearances. It would start with one night, and eventually we were at 4–5 days at a time. He would turn his phone off, go drinking and I wouldn't have a clue what he was at. He would always eventually come back, and in the end I got used to it. Obviously, I was upset, but I had a job to go to, a child to mind and bills had to be paid and looked after. So I would put on a brave face for the world, and the world didn't know the havoc and pain that was inside me. I kept this secret though.

Some writers use the illustration of the seductive and destructive behaviour of the character Don Juan (a legendary character, probably created in the fifteenth century) as an addition to the Jekyll and Hyde image. The modern Don Juan is a womaniser who seduces, but refuses to become emotionally attached, and then abandons the victim. This character is a good example of a person who uses sex as a vehicle of power.

Indeed power and control is the most serious sign that an abusive relationship is on the horizon. It may seem like love, and you feel flattered as the abuser pleads to be always with you. However, if left unchecked, it will soon become constrictive, smothering and intolerable. Your opinions will be disregarded, you will have little input into decision-making, and you will find inequality and unfairness at the core of your relationship.

Your living and breathing space will become confined to the whim of the abuser. Jealousy and suspicion of where you go, and whom you meet, are other warnings of the restrictions that await you, if you persist in this new relationship. There will be hints that may alert you that the abuser is trying at this early stage to isolate you from your friends and family. If you persist with the relationship this will become a reality, as suspicion and jealousy translate into controlling behaviour, and you will experience intense loneliness. That is what happened to Linda. First there was isolation, then the control tightened, and the jealousy and possessiveness emerged as the true face of the nasty Hyde was exposed. Initially, however, Stephen seemed willing to accommodate Linda's desire to live in Galway.

> I had originally lived in Galway and always wanted to return. I suggested it to Stephen but didn't think he would go with it, as it was so far from home. But he did and I was so excited. We purchased a lovely house in Galway. And as it happened, my best friend ended up buying a house in the same area, and was only a few doors down from me. What else could you ask for: a lovely boyfriend that adored you, living in your favourite place, both of us working in jobs we liked and my best friend living down the road? I had my perfect world.

But, that world was soon to change as Stephen plotted his campaign to isolate her. Look at how plausible he was for moving house! It was for the child's sake! No wonder Linda was taken in!

> One day Stephen rang me and told me that a member of his extended family had a house for sale near home. He was so excited about it; he wanted us to think about selling up where we are and move down to where he is from. He said that the house is in the country and we could raise our child in the country and bring the child for walks. He said he would teach the child all about the animals and bring him or her for walks through the fields etc. We would also be nearer to our families than we are now. He said he had no space in our house in town, and wanted a house with room outside for our dogs, and we could have a bigger shed and an easygoing life. So we ended up selling our house, and although we didn't buy the house we had originally planned to buy, we bought one in an isolated part of the countryside. But all I could

see was that maybe this was what he needed, and it would be good for our children to have the freedom of the countryside around the house. I pictured happiness when we bought the house.

Moving to live in a more isolated place is only one stratagem in abusers' plans. Their jealousy and urge to control is so great that they also seek to isolate their partners from friends and family. Some victims, such as Linda, succumb to this devastating abuse for peace sake.

I lost contact with so many friends, through our relationship. The only person I kept in contact with was my best friend, Siobhán. And even at that, I was able to sustain that relationship only because she lived down the road from us and he would nearly always be part of any activities we carried out. Also, she got on with him. All my other friends I lost completely. If he didn't like me around them he would come up with suggestions that they are different to us, or he would belittle a friend's partner. It became easier just to go along with keeping our relationship happy and peaceful, and I left so many friendships behind.

Abusers also try to isolate you psychologically from your family. Stephen made an unsuccessful effort to do this, because Linda is close to her parents, and has a good sense of self-worth, which allowed her to fight to save her marriage, and eventually to leave.

Stephen's disrespect got worse. He began to talk down about my family. We are a close family and I would always talk to my parents about different things in my life that we were doing, and ask their advice. Stephen hated this; he used always say that they are sticking their noses in. He used to slag off my mother in bad ways also. And sometimes he would say to me 'you are just like your mother'.

If you succumb to the blandishments of the charmer, this control will extend very quickly to every aspect of your life, from the clothes you wear to how much you spend.

Frequently, abusers try to make up for their behaviour through sex, another warning sign that is easily missed.

You may feel that you can change the other person and make them into the type of person that you wish them to be. This is a mistaken view, and, as will be seen, even in therapy it is difficult for the abuser to change. You may view the person you love through rose-tinted spectacles, and even ignore the stark warning signpost that your new partner may have been violent in a previous relationship. If it suits, you can even make excuses for a violent temper. This temper may be evident in how they show road rage on a frequent basis, or how they show disrespect and dislike for authority figures. They have an unhealthy competitive nature, and may show spite and criticism of others. The abuser will ridicule, criticise, belittle and judge the opinions of others. He may be kind to you, but show no consideration for the feelings of others. His abusive comments about others may even seem jocose. You will notice that he refuses to listen to others, and behaves like a know-all. Watch for threatening behaviour to others. Pay attention to how he labels them. Above all, watch for the seething anger that arouses fear in those near the hidden volcano.

Some of these behaviours are, on their own, strong signals of an abusive mentality, and if a pattern emerges, you are certainly entering the danger zone of misery, humiliation and control, and possibly of violence. The fact that abuse in long-standing relationships is one of the most prevalent issues that arise in counselling is proof that many people are not aware of these early warning signs, or choose to ignore them because they love the charmer. There are some clear signs attached to a longstanding abusive relationship. The most basic sign is feeling uncomfortable and frustrated, and wondering why you feel this way. You may wonder what is wrong with you. There is always an atmosphere of disgruntlement and anger, and you can never discover why. The abuser denies being angry or else blames you. You often feel upset, frustrated in trying to communicate, and feel misunderstood. You do not feel listened to and find yourself accused of trying to start arguments. The abuser always portrays himself as a victim and you feel guilty, and you are not sure why. Everything you say seems to be wrong, and you may feel unwilling to articulate how you feel, or to challenge the abuse. Lack of healthy boundaries can prevent a person from seeing the true picture. Of course, the type of abuse is also a factor. Emotional abuse is subtle, but domestic violence is evident. Nevertheless, some people in violent relationships do not necessarily see it as abuse. That begs the question if there are people who are easy targets for abusers.

Clients often ask if they are instinctively attracted to people with abusive tendencies, and tend to blame themselves for not seeing abusive behaviours. Repeatedly, they seem to pick the wrong partners. Do abusers, like bullies, see weaknesses that they can exploit in their desire to control? We will later see that women with abusive personality types are sometimes attracted to male abusers, and these form a bilateral (mutual) abusive relationship. But what about those with non-abusive tendencies? Elaine Weiss claims that there is no typical battered woman. How uncomfortable it is to think that we are subject to chance in having a violent or a happy relationship. The abuser may sense exploitable weaknesses in another. He may sense low self-esteem, guilt or gullibility – an easy person to manipulate and control. Therefore, it is essential to recognise what abusive behaviours and attitudes are, so that they can be challenged and an appropriate decision made about the relationship.

As well as being aware of the signs of an abusive relationship, it is helpful to understand the abusive personality and mindset. There are many theories about this, and much controversy about these theories, but those that I find convincing are brain formation and thinking patterns of abusive people. Over the past decade, a large body of research shows that the attachment style of the infant to its mother or primary caregiver wires or programmes the brain. An insecure (fearful or dismissive) attachment, as already discussed in the last chapter, inflicts a neural wound and is imprinted on the brain, laying the pathways for the abusive tendencies in some people. Thankfully, it seems that only a small minority of people who experienced childhood insecure attachment, which is a trauma, become abusers. This tendency can be alleviated if there is someone in the infant's life who meets his emotional needs. Allan Schore, who works in the Centre for Culture, Brain and Development at the Department of Psychiatry and Biobehavioural Sciences at UCLA, explains very well the connection between the biological and psychological interaction in the brain that creates the abusive person. I think that the complexity of this goes a long way to explain how complicated abuse is as a topic for discussion and understanding.

Donald Dutton's book *The Abusive Personality: Violence and control in intimate relationships* is also worth reading on the biological basis for abuse. He explains that the personality type that emerges from an insecure attachment becomes anxious and easily provoked to violence in intimacy. Men who batter see intimate conflict differently from other men, and may feel more threatened, more humiliated, more anxious and angrier. There is a relationship between an insecure attachment and borderline personality disorder (referred to by some psychologists as emotionally unstable personality disorder), so a greater percentage of abusers than non-abusers are also borderline personality. Donald and Deanda Roberts categorise it as an attachment disorder. Borderline personality disorder reflects itself in mood swings, black and white thinking, inability to form warm relationships, and intense rage. There is a strong feeling of abandonment and a consequent urge to control.

The abusive personality type is programmed to control, as a way of easing feelings of being worthless, vulnerable and unlovable. The anger of the person with a propensity for violence is aroused and maintained by thinking distortions, such as making assumptions about a partner without any supporting evidence. These distortions lead the abuser to generalise, to have negative fantasies, and to pick out one aspect of a situation without looking at the whole context.

Lundy Bancroft, in his book *Why Does He Do That? Inside the Minds of Angry and Controlling Men,* accepts that abusers have distorted thinking, but argues that they also plan in a very logical way and conduct a well thought out campaign of torture. Paul Hegstrom's work *Angry Men and the Women who Love Them* points out that abusive people are selective in the targets for their anger. They choose not to control their anger in intimate relationships, but they can do so outside the home. Bancroft argues that beliefs, values and habits are the driving forces of abuse. These beliefs promote feelings of entitlement to special rights or privileges to control and punish. The abuser sees the victim as an unpaid servant, whose role is to nourish him physically, sexually and emotionally, and to treat him with deference. Any failure in this arouses the abuser's anger, and this anger boils, especially if it is the dormant anger arising from an abused childhood. I think I would combine Schore's explanation with Bancroft's to explain more fully the origin of abusive tendencies.

In an abusive household, there are only abusers and victims, and children may learn or internalise this relationship behaviour. As adults, they may prefer the role of abuser in the relationship dynamic, whereby they acquire a sense of control, and escape the pain of being a victim and being at the mercy of another. The entitlement and sense of superiority that an abuser often harbours is a potent sign of disrespect of a partner, which is one of the keystones of the abusive mentality. Linda's husband was enraged when his sense of entitlement was challenged by her father, when the latter heard that she was being abused for the previous year.

> My parents were mad at him. My father was mad that he used to leave me and Jack to fend for ourselves in a house miles away from anywhere for days at a time. They told him that they were not happy about this, and that they will be keeping a close eye on things from now on. Like

any father, my dad wanted to make sure I was ok and was going to keep a check on that. That night Stephen called his mother; I was in bed but I heard the contents of the call. I heard him telling his mother 'Who do they think they are to come to my house and tell me they are going to keep an eye on me and my family'. He then angrily said that if my father ever says anything like that to him again, he would box him.

The beliefs that partly underpin male abusive thinking can also be formed by social and legal influences that undermine respect for women. When I was young in the 1940s and 1950s I learned that a woman's place was in the home, at the kitchen sink, doing menial work. Housework and rearing of children seemed unimportant. For centuries, the law itself militated against the rights of women. In Ireland, the Irish 'mammy' is famous. She waits 'hand and foot' on her beloved sons, and they quickly learn that women are there to love and serve them without any return.

Lundy Bancroft outlines 10 types of abusive personalities who have a predominant type of abusive behaviour in how they mangle the humanity of their victims by power, control, disrespect and demeaning. These can be graded into aggressive and more subtle abusers. Among the aggressive, there is the critical, jealous, violent, dangerous one, whom Bancroft calls the drill sergeant. Another aggressive abuser is the macho and conflictual individual who creates fear, and who sees women as inferior. There is also the abuser who will go to any lengths to inspire fear in his partner. Opposing him is dangerous.

Then there is the gentle, soft-spoken, emotional one who confuses you and makes you feel guilty about hurting his feelings. He blames you, but ignores how you are feeling. Another deceiver is the handsome and sexy abuser, who makes you feel good but increasingly indulges in flirtatious behaviour with other women, making them feel special, and you feel rejected. The victim stance is in all abusers, and this type whines that he has been wronged, especially by women, and that he has a hard life. Among the victim-type abuser is the so-called mentally ill or addictive abuser, who denies responsibility for his actions because of his 'illness' and uses it to make others feel guilty for challenging him. The selfish abuser overvalues his contributions, and sees only his own needs. The know-all abuser, who is an authority on everything, dismisses your contribution with contempt. Finally, there is the calm abuser, who shows contempt for you and quietly demolishes your self-esteem.

Abusers are liars and generally deny their abusive behaviour. Linda's husband, Stephen, never admitted any wrongdoing.

> If he did do something abusive – he generally pretended it didn't happen, and he would never be remorseful for it. He would just pretend that it didn't happen, and it wouldn't be up for discussion. On a few occasions he would deny it to me, and say 'I didn't do that', even though I was the person he did it to. It didn't make any sense whatsoever.

Despite Linda's frequent confrontation, Stephen continued with denial, even when he was having affairs. He refused to move from that stance even when challenged in a couples counselling session.

> I remember asking him to go to counselling when he wanted to reconcile after the affair. He said to me 'we don't need counselling, there is nothing wrong with us'. But there was a lot wrong with us. I had attended counselling for a month or so, while the affair was going on, to get some comprehension of what was happening, or what was going on in my life – or the biggest and most painful question 'WHERE WAS MY LIFE GONE'? He went to counselling though, so that we could give us one last try. He never engaged fully in our sessions, and he just used his comfort angle as a reason for the affair.

While Linda's experiences mirror those of other women, we must not forget that the female abusive personality is similar to the male one. This should not surprise us, since females are as exposed as males to the influences of insecure attachment, childhood abuse and shame. There are, however, biological considerations and differences explored by Allan Schore, which you may like to read. Females with an abusive personality type have many of the characteristics of abusive men, and as adolescents display many features of anti-social behaviour. They harbour an approval of violence, are excessively jealous, distrustful, have poor self-control, and are quick to take revenge. Abusive women are emotionally volatile, have rapidly aroused negative feelings, are easily irritated and are anxious, hostile and tense. They are fearful, have a low stress threshold, are impulsive, and are easily stressed, especially within intimate relationships. They have the same impulse to control as male abusers, and are likely to be involved in sexual, alcohol and drug problems.

Female abusers seek aggressive male companions, and as adults, they tend to form relationships with abusive men and carry out mutual partner violence. Donald Dutton refers to this as bilateral abuse, and reveals that it is much more widespread than might be assumed. Studies show that it can be as high as 45% of abusive relationships. Rates of repeat incidents are far higher than in single perpetrator abuse. Bilateral abuse is particularly strong when couples are addicted to alcohol. Children of such dysfunctional parents have little hope of emerging unscathed into adulthood.

When one partner is violent, the non-abusive victim may retaliate. Self-defence, even of a physical type, is not bilateral abuse.

Controlling others eases the shame the abusers feel. Cradled in shame, they spew it onto other people, especially those closest to them, and use it to humiliate them. Shame is an excruciating experience, and it is impossible to experience fully its pain. It is a deep sense of being flawed that alienates us from ourselves. The most harmful shaming experiences are those that attack the whole self, messages such as 'you are good for nothing', or 'you are a waste of space'. The very young child internalises the shame by identifying with shame-based caregivers, and brings it to adulthood. You can find a more comprehensive exploration of core shame in John Bradshaw's book *Healing the Shame that Binds You*.

Shame also breeds rage, and I strongly believe that rage is part of the powerful mix seen in abusive tendencies. Rage is a primitive emotion, i.e. it appears very early in the child's life, generally in the first eighteen months. This rage can be associated to the intimate relationship between child and mother at that early period. The rage that abusive men show resembles the tantrum of the child at this early period, a primitive response to the possibility of abandonment. The degree of the security of the attachment to the primary caregiver is crucial. It is related in the child's psyche to survival, and any threat to it generates fear, anxiety and rage.

Despite the outpouring of rage and shame, all abusers have a low sense of self-esteem and self-worth, and being in control brings a sense of safety. Abusers feel like victims, and may have been one, so sometimes they carry out the abuse as a way of retribution or revenge. Abusers feel that they are entitled to inflict pain on others. Indeed, they may not even see that they are doing so. They think in extremes and have no concept of boundaries, but tend to over-exaggerate a partner's behaviour. They have a strong intolerance of any type of discomfort, and have rigid beliefs about how a person should be.

The abusive personality type believes the partner is the problem and must be controlled and made subject to his will. He does this by controlling the emotional distance between them. He is determined that she will never be allowed to leave, and that she belongs to him and to no other man. The consequences of this type of thinking can sometimes be fatal, not just to the spouse but to the children also. We often read stories in the newspapers of how families are murdered, and there is no doubt that frequently the abusive personality type is in that sad mix.

Abusive personality types have a dangerous and specific characteristic – the blaming mindset. They project their own negative traits onto their partners. This mindset sees the partner as the source of the abuser's discomfort, shortcomings and failures, and this continually stokes his anger. In Linda's case, the blaming mindset began to tentatively emerge soon after the marriage.

> I was very tired through my pregnancy and didn't have great energy. I was so low in iron I had to get injections. Stephen used to say to me 'I hope when the child is born you will continue to be the same person you were before you got pregnant, and go out'. He said that he hoped I wouldn't turn into one of these boring parents who quieten down when a child comes along. I used to say that I wouldn't get boring, but in the back of my mind I used to think that there would be changes. I was going to be a mother; I couldn't go out and party all night if I wanted to. I would have responsibilities and so would he. Anyway, there were still happy days at this stage. I was married now so I knew we would have to work at it.

The abusive personality very often expresses itself in uncontrolled aggression, has a negative self-view, and is filled with envy and jealousy. The jealousy that he has is an irrational, morbid one fuelled by suspicion, and this is often the most frequently cited motive for spousal murders, and indeed for the suicide of the abuser. This jealousy is not based on love, but on control and the desire to isolate the victim. He often imagines that she is unfaithful, and is driven demented by the thought that his control over her might be loosening. Sometimes in the guise of loving her and wanting to be with her he tries to manipulate her into working in the same place as him. The intense jealousy that Stephen experienced increased throughout his short marriage to Linda, and was accompanied by a stifling possessiveness, a vehicle often used by abusive people to isolate their victims.

At the start, we used to always do things together nearly all the time. No! We did everything together. But throughout the relationship I would want to do things with my friends on my own. I didn't do it much, but on occasion I would go to Christmas parties and other events. There was never a row over it, but there was some tension. It's hard to explain. He just wouldn't be his usual self when I was going to something. He would always warn me never look or talk to any other men. I never did anything throughout our relationship to make him think like this. I was more than 100% committed to him. I used to tell him that he was the one for me, and that no one else compared with him. And I meant it. I never wanted us to part. If things were different, I would have quite happily spent my life with him and I would never have the urge or reason to look at anyone else. But it got to the stage in our relationship that I would be afraid if we were out and some other man talked to me. If we were out together, I would be nervous if I met an old male friend; I know he would be watching, and there would be something about it. So in the end if I did meet someone out that I knew, I would just cut conversation short; it was more important to me at the time that our relationship was happy. I never kept up contact with old friends from home or college.

Even with friends at home, it was the same. I remember one Christmas, when we were out with my parents, and one or two of the lads that I would have known from home were out. Under no circumstances would I go over and talk to them. Even to say hello would have been an issue, and when I did say hello that night to friends living locally, who went to school with me, it was an issue. He would ask, 'Do you like one of them?' He even went as far that night as to say that they kept looking over at us, and that they didn't like him, etc. It was crazy when you think about it. But he could explode if I didn't keep him guaranteed in my behaviour that he was all that mattered. He was *all* that mattered to me, but it was hard to get that into his head.

The abuser's inner world is one of conflict, rage, uncertainty, tensions, paranoia, depression, anxiety and suicidal thoughts. It is interesting that the psychological profile of male batterers is very similar to people diagnosed with Post Traumatic Stress Disorder (PTSD). I will explain this condition later, but the colder and the more rejecting the parents have been, the more severe the trauma symptoms are likely to be. In other words, the more disrupted the attachment of the child, the greater the trauma and the greater the resulting anger and abusive tendencies in adulthood. If a male child is subject to shaming experiences especially by a punitive father, trauma, anger and, for a minority, abusive tendencies may be severely entrenched and magnified. Adolf Hitler is a prime example. Alice Miller's book *For Your Own Good: the roots of violence in child-rearing* gives a fascinating psychological profile of him. All the pent up rage and shame, coming from a childhood where he was regularly savagely beaten and humiliated by his father, were given full vent when he achieved power, and millions died as a result. On a much smaller scale, but on a global level, as the next chapter will show, physical abusers resort to sickening acts of violence to demonstrate power and exert control.

The abuser is needy, and, ironically, the charmer is more often than not a womaniser, who has many affairs. Linda's husband was a serial adulterer, and did not hesitate to use the family home for some of his affairs. She became aware of his infidelity when he brought an ex-partner home one night, when Linda was supposed to be staying at a friend's house. He denied any wrongdoing, and Linda believed him. He then moved in with another woman for a few weeks, and soon began a relationship with a third one.

> When I moved out, he went back into the family home and started another relationship with a girl I knew through other people. Of course, she wasn't local and didn't know the ins and outs of his life. I used to make visits to the house on occasions to give it a quick clean up because it was up for sale. One day I went to our bedroom

to tidy up and what I found was a messy bed, girls' underwear and a set of earrings. It really tore the life from me. This was our marital bedroom. Had he no respect for me or our marriage? But worse was to come. We had a picture of our infant son hanging in our bedroom, and when I looked around, I saw that the picture was gone off the hook. I looked around the room for it. I went into the walk-in wardrobe and there it was hidden under one of his t-shirts. He had taken the picture down, and she obviously didn't know about his child. I still find it hard to come to terms with what I found that day. It made the earrings and underwear seem like small things. My husband had just denied his son to a strange girl he barely knew and for what – to sleep with her. That's how much our son meant. I rang him straight away. He denied it of course, but as I said, the picture was there a few days earlier. It hardly grew legs and walked off the wall! I asked him how he could be so callous, that this was his own flesh and blood, HIS OWN SON! He denied him for his own selfish needs. I don't think now that Stephen ever thought of anyone but himself.

As she writes about the physical, emotional, verbal and financial abuse that she suffered at Stephen's hands, it becomes clear that his infidelity inflicted the greatest hurt of all, because it showed a complete disregard for herself and their child. She found it particularly painful because he had always professed a strong dislike for infidelity.

Many times we talked about it. If he heard of someone being unfaithful, he would say to me how much he hated it, and that if I ever did that to him he would never forgive me. So, because he had such a strong feeling against it, I never believed he would be unfaithful to me. I trusted him in this department 100%. I trusted him totally, when it came to this. I never believed that he would ever do anything like being unfaithful in a million years.

But it is clear that his dislike was at the idea of Linda having an affair. It was part of his control, although she did not realise it at the time. She emphasises the painful impact that his infidelity had on her.

> I was brought to the ground. I felt the worst pain and hurt I have ever experienced in my life. Unbearable pain, a hollow feeling in my stomach every day. I found each day an effort, I used to wake up in the mornings and say to myself sarcastically 'great, another day to work my way through'; I was in total despair. I will never forget these few months as long as I live. I got up in the mornings for my son. That was my only motivation to get up and live. I felt as if I was stripped of every bit of happiness or hope for my future, or even knowledge of where my future was going.

Some three years later when writing her story, that wound is still raw.

> The day I gave my vows at the altar to Stephen, I meant every word with an incredible amount of love. He was the first man that I loved with everything I had. I had never felt so much love towards a man. So I think the unfaithfulness still hurts me today and I think it definitely has left emotional scars on my heart. I write these words, and it hits me like a knife in my stomach – a hollow feeling that only hurt and pain can bring on.

Not only did Stephen bring his mistresses to the family home, he eventually flaunted them in public, causing Linda immense pain. It was a public symbol of abandonment, a flagrant sense of entitlement, and a sign of total irresponsibility as a husband and father. It filled her with confusion as she struggled to understand how a once loving husband could so disregard and distress her. Yet she tried to rationalise his behaviour, and he manipulated her naivety.

> On another occasion, when I had left for a short separation when I couldn't take it anymore, I went to stay with

my parents, and it happened again. This time, though, he was bringing her places with friends of his that knew me. His friend told me what was going on. I remember when I found out that it wasn't a one-night stand but a full-blown affair, I was shattered. I remember specifically hugging my dad one day and asking him to take the pain away. My poor dad felt so helpless. What could he do for me? He was so hurt for me. I still remember that hug with my dad and the feeling I had to this day. I felt so helpless, I felt awful, hurt, shocked and that I had lost total control of my life. I just didn't know what was happening anymore, and that everything I thought my marriage was – wasn't at all. I couldn't understand how Stephen could do this to me. After all he had said about unfaithfulness, here he was doing it. I confronted him about it on the phone, and he didn't deny it. I made excuses for him saying that he didn't know what he was doing; that he was so upset about me going to my parents that he didn't know what to do, and he ran to the first bit of comfort he could get. And, ironically, afterwards when he came back to reconcile these were his words, that he didn't know what he was doing and just wanted some comfort. Yes, but I was hurt also and didn't run to the next man for comfort. I still held my vows to him because I loved him dearly.

You need not be a victim to any of this. By recognising abusive traits early in the relationship, you can avoid great suffering and pain. If you are in an abusive relationship, you can recognise what is going on and begin taking steps to reclaim your life. This, I think, is Linda's wish for you.

To this day, I don't know how many other women have crossed his path. Plenty probably. I just hope one day he doesn't meet a nice girl, and nearly destroy her like he did me! It took a lot of strength and courage to get where I am today! I would never like to see any other person go through it.

Chapter 3

Physical Abuse

I see the snarling ghost of anger
Breathe his fiery breath into my fearful face.
Fetid,
I feel the hurt as angry hand
Violates my precious self
And cower as angry foot
Inflicts its hurt.
And tremble as savage eyes
Penetrate my soul.
How to keep the savage beast
At bay?
To avoid
To avoid
To placate
To placate
To evade
To evade
The monstrous.

Jim O'Shea

Stephen kicked the doors off the wardrobes and presses, and kicked the clotheshorse right across the kitchen. He started wrecking the place and pushing and grabbing me in front of our son in his highchair. The fear I saw in my son's eyes that day still brings a tear to my eye. This was his own father frightening him like this. I felt like this was a film, and couldn't be happening. But it *was* happening.

That is one of several violent episodes of physical abuse by Stephen. Physical abuse is usually the most recognisable and the most difficult abuse to conceal. It is widespread and universal. Ann Jones, in her book *Next Time She'll Be Dead,* states that domestic violence is the leading cause of injury in the United States. Lundy Bancroft reveals that up to 4 million women suffer partner assault each year in the US. Every nine seconds a woman is battered there. When we take the impact on the families of victims, tens of millions of people are affected. Yet domestic violence is the most under-reported crime in America, where only 10% report abuse and only one tenth of family violence defendants are prosecuted. There is no reason to believe that the statistics are different for other countries.

Thangam Debbonaire's extensive study of battering programmes in Ireland shows that there were 10,248 recorded incidents of domestic violence reported to the police in 2002, and only a minority of these resulted in a court conviction. The 2010 MEND (Men Ending Domestic Abuse) report holds that 15% of women and 6% of men in Ireland have experienced severe domestic violence. This is a conservative figure. In Britain, for example, the crime survey of 2005–2006 found that 1 in 20 reported crimes was classified as domestic violence, and 80% of people murdered because of domestic violence were female. In Ireland almost half of all the women killed between 1995 and 2004 were killed by a partner or ex-partner. We know that 140 women have died from domestic violence in Ireland between 1996 and 2007. Between 1967 and 1973, 17,500 women and children were killed by battering men in the US. One third of female homicide victims in the US die from partner violence.

Historically the law did not interfere with family affairs, so spousal assault went unpunished. Even when physical abuse within the family became illegal, police were loath to interfere in what was considered a family matter. This tradition has largely persisted until the present day.

Physical abuse is cyclical insofar as it is passed down from one generation to another. Abuse may also be passed down through cultural practice. Though violent abuse varies from culture to culture and race to race, the core is always power and control, and physical behaviour is used to isolate and trap the victim, leaving her more vulnerable to increased violence. Fortunately, not all children who have witnessed physical abuse become abusers. I believe that emotional warmth and love from the primary caregiver is fundamental to the formation of children, who as adults will be loving caregivers. I have no doubt that a mother can achieve this even in the most abusive circumstances, though it is impossible to fully shield children from the full consequences of the abuse.

Abusive behaviour itself is also cyclical. Dubbed 'the battering cycle', this recognised phenomenon recurs as a pattern within families. Connie Fourré, in her book *Finding Your Way Through Domestic Abuse,* labels abuse as occurring in stages. Stage one is the honeymoon phase, where the abuser is kind and thoughtful, exhibiting the charming behaviour of the abusive personality type. The next stage is characterised by the tension generated when the abuser experiences stress and irritability and becomes cold and distant. The abuser perceives himself as a victim during this stage. Stage three is the crisis phase when the abuser's rage reaches boiling point and is discharged through violence.

Some writers have referred to the cycle as moving from tension building to contrition. Ann Jones sees it as a process of seduction and coercion that confuses the victims. Others depict the abuse as beginning with violence, followed by guilt that he or she may be caught, and then comes rationalisation and excuses, followed by a period of calm and self-control. As the stress of being in an intimate relationship increases, the perpetrator fantasises and plans the next cycle. It is a merry go round whereby the victim is assuaged, loved, belittled, assaulted, and the cycle begins again. Linda's description of the cycle is somewhat muted.

> He used to say to me when he would come back that he didn't know why he done it and he loves us very much and do I know why he was doing this. Now it wasn't like

> I used to just welcome him back with open arms when he
> did come back; I would be really mad with him and tell
> him how much he is hurting and upsetting me and it's
> not fair to do this to me, and I would quiz him about
> where he was. Things would be really nice after one of
> his disappearing acts. When our talks would be over, he
> would go back to the old nice Stephen. But this would
> always be short lived and it wouldn't take long to go back
> to the unpleasant man.

These mind games confuse victims so much that they begin to manifest as battered person's syndrome, the first stage of which is denial. Denying that there is a problem, the victim often makes excuses for the abuser. The second stage is guilt, when she takes on the responsibility for being beaten. She becomes part of a codependent relationship where she strives to be a 'better' wife, mother, and so on, hoping in vain that this will prevent the violence. The third phase, enlightenment, occurs when the victim realises that no one deserves to be beaten, but remains in the abusive situation in the hope the relationship will change for the better. The final stage is called responsibility, because the victim realises that only the abuser can heal himself. To manage this stage successfully, the victim must take the necessary steps to leave the abusive relationship, a move that will be explored later.

Research shows that some people batter (strike repeatedly) to exert power and control for three reasons – to get their partners to stop doing something they disapprove of, to stop them from saying things or to end an argument, and to punish them for something they have done.

As we have seen, this desire for power and control is fuelled by the seething furnace of rage and shame. Think of the vulnerable and raging abandoned child crouched in the psyche of the seemingly charming adult. When the conquest is over, he is ready to strike. There is no rage as intense as the rage of the child, but when it has the weapon of adult physical strength, how dangerous it can be in intimate relationships.

Male batterers are the victims of socialisation. Boys at a young age have traditionally been taught to hide their sadness and pain, and to respond to stress without showing emotion. Men are more likely to feel anger, but before anger emerges, they will have experienced hurt, rejection, humiliation, loneliness, helplessness, and so on. When these are suppressed, they turn into anger. Sometimes anger becomes addictive, and batterers find relief by striking out. This then becomes a pattern of relief and release. Male children who witness violence among their parents are 700 times more likely to become batterers, and if they have been physically abused, are 1,000 times more likely to beat their female partners.

Physical abuse violently breaches safety boundaries, humiliates the victim, and demeans the abuser. In an earlier chapter, we saw the skin as our most basic boundary. Physical abuse is a blatant and evident battering of this boundary, as is any physically aggressive behaviour, withholding of physical needs, indirect physical harm, or the threat of physical abuse.

Physically abusive behaviours are accompanied by verbal and psychological abuse that leaves mental as well as physical scars. The movie *The Burning Bed*, starring the late Farrah Fawcett, graphically illustrates this behaviour. It was adapted from the non-fiction book by Faith McNulty about a battered housewife, Francine Hughes, who set fire to her husband's bedroom as he lay in a drunken sleep. The story is told in flashback by Francine, starting from the time she met her husband at a dance in 1963 until the night of the murder in 1977. The abuse follows the typical cycle discussed earlier, but eventually degenerates into unremitting abuse. The movie was traumatic for Farrah, who was also in a physically abusive relationship at an earlier stage of her life.

Victims' stories in Elaine Weiss's work also exhibit many instances of physical abusive behaviours. Some describe how abusive partners inflicted pain and fear without leaving any visible signs of abuse. One emotionally detached and immensely cruel husband placed a pillow over his wife's face as she slept. The following day, he acted as if nothing had happened. Though he never left any marks of his physical violence, he inculcated the fear that is the hallmark of violence perpetuated by men against women. Sandra Horley, the Chief Executive of Refuge (a UK network of safe houses providing emergency accommodation for abused women and their children), was prompted to write her book *Power and Control: why charming men can make dangerous lovers* because of one woman, whose life was hell for twenty-five years but whose husband never hit her. She also tells how one abusive husband kept a knife by the bed, and another an axe under the pillow. These are deliberate acts, carefully thought out to instil fear, and clearly illustrate that abuse is not about anger *per se*, but is managed and is about power and control.

Other women tell stories that show violence that is more obvious. Weiss's book contains stories of women knocked unconscious by blows to the face sufficiently powerful to send them hurtling across the room. Another story reveals how a man scratched his name on different parts of his wife's body. Even when she had fled from him, these marks, the most personal sign of power and ownership, were a constant and fearful reminder of her ordeal. One survivor sustained permanent injury to the ligaments of her arm when her husband viciously twisted it behind her back. Another was constantly beaten, her arm and nose were broken, her ribs cracked, and one of her kidneys ruptured. After one beating, she was in a coma for several weeks and had multiple brain haemorrhages. Ann Jones gives examples of horrendous injuries, including one of a female victim whose face was permanently disfigured by a violent partner. Sandra Horley relates how an abusive husband cut off his wife's beautiful hair with a knife and gloated about how ugly she was.

In her story, Linda sometimes minimises the physical abuse, especially when it was not directed specifically at her. Driven by envy, jealousy and rage, Stephen's violent tendencies erupted on the night that she left her job in Galway, when her company treated her to drinks and praised her work ethic. When Stephen arrived home his rage was in full flow, and he attacked the car, tearing off the wipers and smashing the mirrors. When they moved to their more remote house, the violence became more terrifying, and was directed at her. Again, she is inclined to minimise this, although in retrospect she realised that it would get worse, because she knew that his father battered his mother. Despite the violence she tried to keep it secret, which is one of the characteristics of victims' behaviour.

One of the earlier memories she has of physical abuse was when

> Stephen pushed me to the couch when I was pregnant. He was leaving again, and I knew he was going to go drinking for the night. I stood in front of him and pleaded with him not to go, but he just shoved me out of his way. I was about 7–8 months pregnant at that time.
>
> Stephen never punched or kicked me, but he threw things at me. I remember one Sunday, when we had just moved to our new house, he was in the pub, and I rang him and told him to come home. I explained that I needed help with Jack, and told him that if he didn't come up from the pub and help me out, I was going down there, and in front of everyone I would ask him to leave. I was at the end of my tether with him; I was just after having our child who was a few weeks old. I was exhausted and he was giving no help. Of course, it was the worst thing I could have done; he came home in a rage, and threw the toaster at me. He then stormed out of the house and went back drinking. I didn't see him until the following evening.
>
> Another vivid memory was the night we went out with my cousin and her husband. His rage showed that night too. He started drinking, and we went from one venue to another. On the way, he disappeared. I didn't know where he had gone, and tried ringing his phone, but there was no answer. I made excuses to my cousin that he would be back. I said that he must have met someone

along the way and that we must have kept walking along and missed him. After a while, we gave up and decided to get a taxi home. We were on the side of the street trying to get the taxi, when we saw him walk towards us. He walked straight to me, and with the most intense strength pushed me so hard I went flying back on my back, and banged my head off the kerb. He then ran off. I remember a passer by saying 'that is just unbelievable what he has just done to that girl'. My cousin was livid and told him she was going to the gardaí over this. What was more shocking and unbelievable to me was that he could do this to me – number one – for nothing. And he did it in public right in front of my cousin. I remember feeling so embarrassed, because my cousin had no idea of the way things were. She only knew what I told her, which was that everything was great. I swore her to secrecy regarding that event, and told her I didn't want her telling anyone. Of course, she quizzed me, and asked me to consider leaving him. I told her that there must be something upsetting him, and that it was the first time he had done such a thing. I said that I would talk to him, and that he feels really bad. He got up the next day and pretended it didn't happen, when my cousin was gone home.

As I said he never punched or kicked me, but sometimes he would charge at me in a rage, when he would push or shove me. The expression on his face made me afraid. He put his arm around my neck one day just to frighten me.

It may be difficult for those who have never experienced abuse to believe that such barbarous acts can happen in an intimate relationship. However, the list of physical abuse is long and horrifying. Physical abusers strike, punch, shove and slap. They may hit their victims with objects or throw objects at them. They may resort to pinching, kicking and even strangling. Others instil fear by trying to drown victims, they confuse them by depriving them of sleep, and they expose them to cold, or burn them. Abusers torture their victims by electric shock, tying them up, and threatening to shoot them. Some unfortunate victims are exposed to toxic substances, infected with a disease, or deprived of food and medication. The list could go on.

Physical abuse is not defined only by violent behaviour. Violence is any act that engenders fear. It is about striking terror into victims to make them easier to control. This may mean attacking objects in their presence, for example hitting or kicking walls and doors during an argument, throwing things in anger, and destruction of property or, like Stephen, tearing the mirrors off a car. The marks left on walls or property, and the smashed wipers and mirrors are concrete, constant reminders of control and violence that make the victim feel unsafe. Many years ago I was in a house with large holes in the internal doors, indicating the presence of violent behaviour. It was a chilling experience for me. How much more fearful for the victim!

One particularly awful type of physical abuse is the use of pets to control and arouse fear. Perpetrators often torture their partners' pets. The implied threat is 'I can kill your pet, and I can kill you if necessary'. A client of Lundy Bancroft described how her partner illustrated in detail how he was going to torture and kill her cat. One of Elaine Weiss's narrators watched in horror and fear as her pet was being choked, its eyes bulging as it struggled to escape.

For me the most unspeakable and common form of abuse is the abuse of pregnant women. Another recoverer recounted to Elaine Weiss how her husband kicked her when she was pregnant. Physical abuse of a pregnant woman may damage the foetus, and there is plenty of evidence of miscarriages, still-births and foetal deaths due to such violence. A miscarriage in itself can be a traumatic event, giving rise to intense feelings of loss and extreme loneliness. How much worse is the loss exacted by the savagery of an intimate partner? Christiane Sanderson, in her book *Counselling Survivors of Domestic Abuse*, draws attention to the fact that injuries around the breast and abdomen indicate that the abuser directs his rage towards the baby as well as towards his mother. This monstrous behaviour is considered so serious and so common that the Public Health Agency of Canada has set up the Canadian Perinatal Surveillance System (CPSS) to prevent or limit it.

Physical abuse is not only confined to intimate relationships, but to all relationships. Elderly people are also vulnerable to abuse. Approximately 6% of the elderly population suffer abuse. The Irish Health Service Executive (HSE) indicates that 37% of referrals for elder abuse were on behalf of men and 63% on behalf of women in 2007. Some 35% were substantiated and 42% remained inconclusive. The data collected was incomplete because the data collection processes had not been fully developed until 2008, but they show that at least 14% of elder abuse is physical, a number that matches international statistics.

Imagine you are a 90-year-old person confined to a nursing home. Imagine how frail you feel. Your physical strength has gone. Your eyesight is failing. You no longer have any interest in reading. You are dependent on others even for a drink of water. Imagine you have dementia or Alzheimer's. You have regressed to childhood. You want to go home to see your mother, your father, or your grandmother. Imagine how helpless you are. Unable to defend yourself. Physical abuse of the vulnerable highlights how cowardly abusers are. It is difficult to believe that people assault, mug, beat, whip, punch and slap elderly people. There are many instances of the elderly being choked, kicked, pinched, bitten, and spat at. Cases have occurred of old people being subjected to force-feeding, hair pulling, and even burning. We often hear about elderly people being restrained inappropriately and manhandled when moved. Carers overmedicate to render them incapable of being 'troublesome', and impose curfews as punishment.

The Irish Health Service Executive estimates that at least 20% of elderly people suffer from physical neglect that includes lack of supervision or monitoring, inappropriate housing, inadequate provision of food and water, lack of assistance with eating or drinking, insufficient clothing for the weather, and abandonment. Add to this list delays in receiving medical assistance, careless administration of medicines, lack of help with hygiene or bathing, incorrect body positioning that leads to skin damage, and lack of help for mobility. Neglect can also include lack of access to a toilet, ignoring requests to be taken to the toilet, inadequate changing of diapers, and so on. Many of these abuses are particularly relevant to nursing homes. Those dealing with the elderly in nursing homes should respect them and love them, however difficult and cranky some may be. Irish people have been outraged by recent media revelations of elderly people suffering physical and other types of abuse by home care providers, who are grant-aided by the Health Service Executive. Concerns about lack of training, vetting and regulation of these companies have been well aired in the media. Abuse is not only about power and control, but also about respecting the person's humanity, and in the cases highlighted, the elderly were shown scant respect.

Indicators of elder physical abuse include sprains, dislocations, fractures, and broken bones. However, it is important to look for patterns or clusters of indicators because some of these signs may be the outcome of accidents, and not abuse. Burns from cigarettes or hot water, and abrasions on the arms, legs or torso that resemble rope or strap marks are particularly noteworthy. The following bruises are rarely accidental: bruising on both arms or both inner thighs, wrap around bruises that encircle the arms, legs or torso (indicating physical restraint), multicoloured bruises (indicating that they were sustained over time), and signs of traumatic hair and tooth loss. Expressions of pain and difficulty with normal functioning of organs may indicate internal injuries.

Thankfully, elder abuse is generally no longer occurring under the radar, although another common type of physical abuse is rarely mentioned. It is the abuse and intimidation of entire families in a social setting. 'Neighbours from hell' are master abusers, and intimidate, for example, by pulling shrubs, invading property, kicking footballs at a neighbour's house or at the neighbour, damaging a neighbour's car, shouting, and playing loud music late at night. They sometimes succeed in making neighbours so fearful that they remain confined to their house. They copper-fasten their neighbours' isolation by slandering them to other residents on an estate, and blaming them for all confrontations. This is exactly what happens in an intimate relationship, where the abuser tries to isolate the victim.

Physical abusers do not accept responsibility for their behaviours, but blame others for their own feelings, by making such statements as 'you make me mad', 'I wouldn't feel like this if it weren't for you', and so on. Since abusers have low self-esteem, they are hypersensitive and easily insulted or upset. They perceive small setbacks as serious personal injustices, and react accordingly.

Some male abusers appear to show remorse and conscience, but it is hard to see how genuine this is, since the basic mindset of the abusive personality type neutralises any feelings of guilt or compassion. For example, they minimise battery by saying that it happens only occasionally, or that they did not use a weapon and so the abuse is not really bad. They argue that spousal abuse happens in all relationships. Others use moral justification, citing scripture to show that a wife should submit to the (male) head of the household.

Pleading lack of control from drunkenness is also a common excuse. One of the worst ways of diminishing the horror of physical abuse is to dehumanise the victim by saying that the abused person deserves everything she gets.

Much of the above evidence relates to male violence against women, but since the female abusive personality type is similar to the male one, it should come as no surprise to learn that women are as physically abusive as men. There are many statistics among researchers with, however, significant different outcomes. So it is unsurprising that statements about the extent of female perpetration arouse some controversy. Irrespective of statistics, it is now recognised by state institutions and state health bodies that men suffer abuse at the hands of women. Dr Martin Fiebert, a clinical psychologist at California State University, has recently published a substantial list of reliable sources on female abuse. A 1970s report indicates that men suffer as much physical violence at the hands of women as women do from men. Almost 40–50 % of men will suffer physical abuse, a statistic comparable to women victims. Joy Stevens quotes from a 1997 survey of dating couples in which 30% of the women admitted beating their partners. Not all female assaults are retaliation against male violence, but arise from a need for power. This is clearly seen in lesbian relationships, where perpetrators show similar characteristics of dependence and jealousy as male abusers.

Physical abuse of men by women is also grossly underreported. Women are ten times more likely to call the police than men. Interestingly, the main reason men do not report abuse is to protect their partners. Furthermore, they rightly feel that health professionals and police are less likely to believe them. Justice systems are more likely to accept that the male is the aggressor. On the other hand, there is clear evidence that male perpetrators of domestic violence generally inflict far greater injuries, and certainly more fatalities. They also arouse greater fear in the victims. Marianne Hester draws attention to the fact that men are more likely to be repeat offenders.

In the final analysis, abuse is always wrong, and should always be condemned, irrespective of gender. Male victims should report abuse as readily as females. Every effort must be taken by both men and women to address the appalling impact of physical abuse on its victims.

Christiane Sanderson outlines the full impact of this abuse, which is too comprehensive to discuss fully here. In addition to physical scars and long-term physical ailments like arthritis, hearing problems, stress, brain damage, ulcers, indigestion and headaches, victims may also experience depression, obsessive compulsive disorder, suicide and substance abuse. Physical abuse (along with sexual abuse) is one of the main causes of self-harm, or cutting, which will be briefly explored in the chapter on child abuse. Victims are so confused by the abuse that they blame themselves and lose their perspective. They are enveloped in feelings of self-doubt and worthlessness. Physically abused men feel anger, a desire for revenge, and shame. A small number experience fear.

Some physically abused women, traumatised by years of violence, lose their sense of self. They experience nightmares, shame, and symptoms of Post Traumatic Stress Disorder. PTSD is a serious anxiety complaint consisting of flashbacks, hypervigilance, and a heightened startle response. Sufferers are easily stressed. They experience intense panic, fear and terror. They have difficulty in sleeping, and they suffer nightmares. They risk becoming depressed and withdrawn. They are wracked by sadness, anger, guilt, pessimism and fatigue. Some sufferers of PTSD become emotionally numb, and may experience sexual problems. Many experience physical aches and pains.

Reading about the impact of physical abuse can be difficult, but talking to someone who has been battered is even more gruelling. When I see the tear-stained faces of my clients I get a better understanding of the devastation of physical abuse. I hope that as people become better educated about physical abuse and its consequences, they will be more inclined to take the necessary measures to confront and defeat it.

Chapter 4

Verbal Abuse

Nurtured in the furnace of shame,
The abuse-foetus grows,
Silent,
Strong
And lies in wait,
Fed on the poison of rejection,
Never good enough,
Never loved enough,
Unlovable,
And then it stirs
And Strikes,
And paralyses.
And leaves the eternal scar.
Hidden.

How it rings eternally in your ear,
Bringing fear at your worthlessness,
Becoming the inner negative voice,
Reminding you of your uselessness,
Eternally labelled stupid and incompetent,
Hardly fit to inhabit the space you take.
Your soul bows before the onslaught,
A tree in the eye of the storm,
The wounding hail that stings,
Before the calm
Returns.

Jim O'Shea

Unlike physical abuse, verbal abuse is not illegal, except perhaps in the context of workplace bullying or defamation. It is,

however, lethal in its destructive power. No wonder St James writes about the tongue, and how this small bodily member can inflict such huge hurt! A tiny spark can destroy an entire forest! This is well illustrated in Patricia Evans' books, *The Verbally Abusive Relationship* and *Verbal Abuse: survivors speak out*, which are worth reading for a more comprehensive understanding of verbal abuse. Verbal abuse is so tormenting because the facility to praise and express love is used to denigrate and insult. For example, Linda went from being a beautiful desirable wife to a 'boring old hag'. The contrast is devastating, and the constant name-calling savage.

> I was called things like a 'bitch', a 'cunt'. These seemed his favourite names to call me. He would tell me to 'fuck off' so many times. I used to plead with him not to call me those names; he would say this to me in front of his son from his previous relationship, who was old enough to understand what he was saying. He also said it in front of my son – even though he was too young to know what he was saying, I really used to fear that day when my son would understand what he was saying. In addition, if my son saw daddy saying these things to mammy then he would think it was o.k. to say this – and what if the day came that my son called me one of the above! I really think that would destroy me.

Linda is right. Jack would learn this form of malignant communication. We all remember those verbal barbs at ourselves that entered our souls at an early stage. Perhaps a parent, a so-called friend or a teacher spoke them. Long ago in the schoolyard I often heard the slogan 'sticks and stones may break my bones, but names will never hurt me'. It sounded reasonable then, but I now realise that it is a myth. Many clients have told me that names have hurt them far more than broken bones. One of Elaine Weiss's narrators, who endured horrible physical abuse, maintains that the verbal abuse she suffered was worse than the physical. Its impact lasted for years. We never forget the sarcasm, nicknames or words of scorn thrown at us in childhood or adulthood. Verbal scars remain etched on our souls, and research supports the view that they are more damaging than physical or emotional abuse.

Lundy Bancroft, an expert on abusive men, contends that the behaviour of verbal and physical abusers grows from the same roots, and that verbal abuse normally precedes physical assault. The abuser uses verbal put downs and insults to degrade and depersonalise the victim, so that the physical abuse can be minimised and rationalised. When the abuser no longer sees the victim as human, he can justify the violence and evade remorse. To avoid responsibility for their actions and words, verbal abusers also refuse to talk about upsetting issues that the victim wishes to discuss.

Education increases the facility abusers have with words. They have a rapier-like capacity to inflict verbal abuse, some of it extremely subtle. As Cathy Meyer says, not all words meant to hurt are ugly words. An 'expert' at verbal abuse can damage the self-esteem of another, and yet appear to care deeply for them. They frequently use the phrases 'What's the matter with you?' or 'I don't know what you're talking about'. Further, the victim can be utterly confused by verbal abuse because the abuser sometimes appears vulnerable, lost, loving or supportive, until the blaming begins again.

There are many stories of verbal abuse in the book *Wounded by Words*, written by Susan Osborn and her colleagues. These stories describe the blaming, belittling, isolation, indoctrination, shaming, escalating control, silencing, rejection and insults that accompany verbal abuse. Abusers like to degrade others by swearing at them, calling them stupid, shouting at them, insulting them and imitating them. These individuals are shamers, who use criticism, sarcasm and mocking words to degrade their victims. Some abusers are very volatile and resort to yelling, swearing or screaming with little provocation. As with all abusers, they blame the victim for their actions, alleging that if the victim were only 'perfect' the abuser would not lose control. Verbal abusers are quick to threaten. These threats indicate that violence is imminent. Threats are used to control or to influence victims' behaviours. This can occur in the context of a divorce, especially when the abuser wishes to stay in the marriage. Overall, they coerce their victims to follow their way of thinking, regardless of how harmful it is to them.

Patricia Evans categorises the controlling behaviours of verbal abusers. One abusive type withdraws from intimacy, eschews empathy, and dismisses a partner's desperate need to be heard. How often have I heard some of my clients say 'he/she never listens to me. It's as if I don't exist.' These abusers remain bunkered inside their rigid boundaries and refuse to engage in any meaningful dialogue. They dismiss their victim's plea for understanding and discussion. Ironically, such insidious abusers may be perceived by others as quiet, gentle individuals, a passivity that utterly confuses the unfortunate victim and plays with the mind. Yet anger always simmers beneath the calm surface. It is more apparent in aggressive verbal abusers, who make serious threats to harm the victim and to engender fear. They may threaten to abandon the victim, or to kill her and her children, unless she does what he wishes.

Verbal abusers use all their verbal skill to confuse, control and disarm their victims. They are blatantly unfair, they rule out any opposing viewpoint, and they make the victim feel stupid. They distort the victim's judgement and make them feel that there is something wrong with them. They make statements like 'you have no sense of humour', 'you are too soft', 'grow up', 'you have no common sense', 'you have a big mouth', and so on. Sometimes they humiliate in a humorous or sarcastic way. This denigration will reinforce any pre-existing low self-worth engendered in the victim during childhood.

Victims of verbal abuse find that they have no say in any discussion with their abuser. They may wish to discuss something, but the controlling abuser prevents communication, using dismissive remarks such as 'you know nothing about this', 'that's ridiculous', or 'I don't wish to talk about that'. Such dismissal is painful when one's need to communicate is stifled and controlled. This hurt and confusion are magnified by the judgemental attitude of the verbal abuser, who blames the victim for arguments, or uses subtle phrases to make him or her feel small and stupid. I have met victims whose abusers denied their blatantly abusive behaviour.

I mentioned in a previous chapter that abusive personality types feel entitled to do as they wish with their victims, and to exert full control over them. They dictate how the victims should live, what they should wear, and how they should behave. Verbal abusers make snide remarks about the victims' clothes, views and behaviours. Indeed as anger builds up inside the verbal abuser, he or she will strike with venomous words, in much the same way as a physical abuser strikes. This striking out is the angry and vicious verbal assault of the tiny abandoned child in the powerful adult body.

Normally verbal abuse occurs in a private setting, although it can happen in public, where it is often expressed non-verbally. Non-verbal abuse resembles emotional abuse. These non-verbal messages include gestures, frowns, narrowing of the eyes, lifted eyebrows, scowls, sneering expressions, threatening expressions, and body movements. Frowning, for example, conveys a warning and a message of fear to the victim of what may be in store in a more private setting. It conveys the abuser's anger and displeasure.

The effects of verbal abuse are serious, and like all cases of abuse become more intense over time. Recovery from verbal abuse seems to take much longer than from physical abuse, because the core self is assaulted and wounded. It often happens that the victim becomes used to and adapts to abusive behaviours. Verbal abuse can have physical effects. Sarah Osborn reveals that she developed ulcers and hair loss because of it. On a psychological level, verbal abuse reduces the victims' self-esteem and makes them feel worthless. Victims often internalise the criticisms, and come to believe that they are true. They begin to accept that they are worthless and unlovable. I sometimes ask my verbally abused clients to draw an ear and write down the negative messages that were directed at them. The results are horrifying, and reflect the actions of unfeeling and distant parents or partners.

Ironically, the more victims see themselves as worthless and unlovable, and the more they feel fearful, sad, powerless and indecisive, the more they may cling to the abuser because he/she pays some attention to them. They sink into depression and lose their creativity. They feel flawed. They experience a sense of unhappiness and mistrust. People who suffer continuous verbal abuse lose their good judgement, doubt themselves, and wonder what they are missing. Happiness is an elusive dream. They want to escape from their chaotic prison by not living in the present, which is too painful, yet they are unable to trust in future relationships.

Prolonged verbal abuse makes victims feel crazy, partly because the abuser determines their boundaries. They are deprived of ownership of their feelings, thoughts and behaviours. Confusion is part of feeling crazy and is one of the main results of abuse. In the early days of grieving over my dead child, I experienced what feeling crazy is like. I felt lost, disconnected, restless, disorientated, empty and confused. This is how victims of verbal abuse feel. They also feel cowed and fearful of challenging the abuser to clarify their muddled thoughts. They feel constricted, shackled, and puzzled about what is happening.

As they struggle in confusion, victims often form a false set of beliefs, such as believing that they might appease the abusers if they were better at articulating what they wished to say. Abusers reinforce these false beliefs by convincing them that they are incapable of understanding, and that if they could correct this they would not provoke anger. When they see their abuser behaving kindly and courteously to others, they become convinced that they are at fault, and that something must be wrong with them. These beliefs show how victims take responsibility for the abuse, and come to doubt every aspect of themselves, as their personality is dismantled.

If you commit to a verbal abuser, this, too, will be your lot. Your initially marvellous relationship will deteriorate over time, and love and trust will be stillborn. You will find yourself in a codependent relationship, where you inadvertently nourish the abuser by trying to please him. You will find yourself on a treadmill of short-lived happiness and prolonged hurt in the cycle of abuse. As your anger grows at the prospect of a life ruined, your relationship may change from codependency to mutual abuse. You will be neglected emotionally and physically. You will be subject to bouts of jealousy by your abusive partner as the noose of control tightens around your neck and you lose contact with your friends and family.

Perhaps you are in a verbally abusive relationship and you do not realise it. Dr Irene Matiatos, an American psychologist, might enlighten you with some of the questions she proposes. Are your feelings ignored and ridiculed? Do you feel disrespected and dismissed? Perhaps you never receive appreciation and affection and you are treated coldly. Are you berated, shouted at, or subject to unpredictable mood swings? Are your beliefs, opinions, class and religion ridiculed? Are you left speechless with anger as your partner walks away without answering you? Does he use your justified anger as an excuse to blame you for the problem? He is right and you are wrong! You are too sensitive, you do not understand him, you are unfaithful, none of the abuse you complain of is happening!

Perhaps your partner humiliates you in private and in public, and makes it difficult for you to socialise with your friends and family. Perhaps he makes you socialise when you prefer to stay at home or are not feeling well. His control may extend beyond this to all the decisions affecting your home and relationship, including how you dress. If you complain, does he come across as the victim? Does he then exact revenge by hurting you when you are ill or down, or by twisting your words and turning them against you? Does he threaten to abandon you or to hurt you or your family? Does he manipulate you with lies and make you feel useless? Perhaps you are terrified as your partner drives like a maniac or is frequently subject to road rage. You will notice that as you become exhausted by trying to defend yourself, his anger energises him, as he creatively finds other ways to torture you. Are you mollified and gratified later when he promises that he will never hurt you again? Until the next time, that is!

Your own behaviours may also indicate that you are being abused. Do you feel muzzled or fearful of expressing your opinions to your partner? Do you feel emotionally unsafe, insecure and vulnerable? Do you doubt your own judgements and capabilities? Are you afraid to speak to others about your relationship? Do you make excuses for your partner's behaviour? You long for the softer side of your partner. You fantasise about it, hoping that it will become a reality if you make every effort to show love and understanding. If you constantly feel down, experience little joy or excitement, or if you feel powerless, confused and trapped, you may be in an abusive relationship. Look at Linda's experience as she struggled in a web of abuse, and notice how she swore her sister to secrecy.

> At this stage I began to feel TRAPPED! What was happening I had no idea! How had my life become like this? What had happened to us? Why was he being like this? We were his family; did he not care about us? I felt I was in so deep at this stage that I couldn't contemplate getting out! Yes, it ran through my mind sometimes, but it was a fantasy more than anything real. I had a son, marriage, house with a mortgage, and bills. I felt I was going nowhere. But I knew I wasn't happy, and that my life was passing by each day with work, chores, sadness and worry. One day when it all got too much I confided in my sister, but swore her to secrecy. I remember standing in the corner of the kitchen telling her I feel trapped –

ironically, I felt like I was in a corner in my life. One I
couldn't get out of, or see a solution to.

Another way to recognise if you are in a verbally abusive relationship is to evaluate if your basic rights and needs are
being met. You have a basic right and need to be respected,
to be listened to with courtesy, and to have emotional support. You are entitled to have a different opinion to your
partner, to have your feelings acknowledged, and to receive
an apology if you have been insulted. You should rightly expect kindliness and encouragement from your partner, and,
of course, you are entitled to live free from fear, anger, threat,
criticism, accusation, blame or judgement. You are entitled to
be an equal partner in the relationship, rather than an inferior subordinate.

Because victims are reduced to feeling helpless and worthless, many find it very difficult or impossible to confront verbal
abuse. They must begin by acknowledging the abuse.
Frequently they only realise that they are being abused when it
is pointed out to them in counselling, or perhaps by a friend or
family member. Until then it has been a normal way of living,
but they come for counselling because they feel that something
indefinable is wrong with them. They cannot make sense of
how they feel, and many are shocked when I mention that they
are being abused in a codependent relationship.

I have already looked at codependency in the context of
boundaries, and Melody Beattie, in her book *Codependent No
More*, offers suggestions to people who are codependent.
Firstly, you must break your obsession with your partner and
detach. This is not a cold, calculated behaviour or a withdrawal
of love or concern, but detaching from an entanglement and a
responsibility that is not yours. It is releasing a burden, becoming free, and giving up the vain quest to rescue. I believe it is
disrespectful to take on the responsibilities of others, and can
become an enmeshment of boundaries. It takes away your
partner's power and potential, and can lead to mutual anger.

Being codependent is a terrible prison, and you may wish to get a more comprehensive knowledge of it by reading Melody's book.

However, abuse cannot be minimised. Even if the abuse is subtle and coated with charm, it always makes the victim feel uncomfortable. Naming it makes it more concrete and therefore more visible. When it has been identified, it should be calmly confronted, and firmly and directly rebuffed. This demands an assertiveness the victim may lack. Nevertheless, sometimes it is too dangerous to confront a verbal abuser, who may resort to violence if challenged. In such cases, the victims must make choices. They can choose to stay in the abusive relationship and cope with it as best they can, or choose to leave.

Some writers outline tactics to counteract verbal abuse while remaining in the abusive relationship, but I am unwilling to highlight anything that might encourage anyone to remain in an abusive situation. Few counsellors help clients to remain in an abusive environment. I believe in confronting the abuse, and if it does not cease, escaping it. Leaving the prison of an abusive relationship can be extremely difficult. When children are involved, it demands much soul searching and preparation, which I will explore in another chapter.

Chapter 5

Emotional/Psychological Abuse

She grew close to him
And felt the warmth of his love
Enveloping her in its gentle embrace.
She did not feel the chill
That sometime came
And brushed against the edges of her soul.
Looking with sightless eye,
He did not see
The cut inflicted on her soul.
A silent gash
That deeply wounded self,
And left mind confused
And spirit lifeless.

Jim O'Shea

There are many rather vague definitions of emotional abuse, and so I will tell you a short true story, which contains the essential ingredients of this type of abuse, and which will show the emotional abuser as a moody, sulky, individual, who infects the atmosphere of a household with sourness, hostility and bad humour. Alex told me this story. He and his wife, Joan, spent four months with his parents, while awaiting the completion of their new house. They had three small children, and Joan was pregnant with their fourth child, when she was subject to a campaign of intimidation and cruelty.

> I was delighted when my mother welcomed us with open arms. We hadn't much money, and staying with them for three months would save us a lot. After a few weeks, Joan

64

began to tell me of strange changes in my mother's behaviour. She was all smiles when people called to the house, but when they were alone her face darkened and she would go about in silence. Joan found this very difficult, and felt that we weren't wanted. I told her this was nonsense; my mother was a very welcoming person. She was known as such by many. Joan grew more distressed when my mother began to tell my father that Joan was hiding the house keys. This went on day after day, and my father was tormented by it all. Then she began to spread lies about Joan. She told neighbours that Joan was sitting about all day, while she herself was exhausted doing all the housework. One nosey neighbour told Joan that she should be helping my mother, and not the other way round. Joan became angry, and went on about it every evening when I came home from work. I couldn't believe it at first, but I began to realise that my mother was telling lies, and that it was she who was hiding the keys, and it was she who was sitting around acting the martyr. Eventually I exploded, and the four of us had a huge row one night. My father believed my mother, and I believed Joan. There was a real shouting match, and I felt strong hatred for my mother. But my mother's behaviour stopped after this, and anyway we moved into our new house soon after, but the damage was done, and I felt so angry with her for a long time. I think my father was afraid of my mother.

The 2007 report of Women's Aid, an Irish organisation that assists abused women, shows that reports of emotional or psychological abuse were greater than any other type of abuse. The same is true for Canada and the United States. All classes, races, genders and ages are targets for emotional abuse. In his book *Healing the Scars of Emotional Abuse*, Gregory Jantz holds that emotional abuse can be inflicted through words, actions, neglect and spirituality.

Linda's story reflects this. Stephen ignored her pleas to converse with her. It was as if she did not exist, or did not matter. He let her know that watching TV was more important to him than talking to her. He used silence, insults or blaming to defeat her.

> Stephen was never really interested in my conversations about any item I would bring up. He would look at the TV and barely answer me. Sometimes I would sit on the couch beside him and wait for him to respond, and eventually say, 'Are you going to respond?' He never had interest in these conversations.
>
> He had a brick wall around him and he would raise it around him anytime I tried to talk about our issues, and so things got worse and worse. Sometimes when I tried to talk to him about our problems he would imitate me with his hands and say 'blaa blaa do you ever shut up?' The first time he said that to me I told him not to talk to me like that, and say, 'Who do you think you are talking to' but he would tell me 'fuck off', and leave the house.
>
> I didn't feel one bit loved or cared for. A gap began to grow between us and it grew bigger and bigger. He used to say to me "we are like two people sharing a house". I would respond, 'how can you expect me to be intimate or close to you, you hurt me every other week with your disappearing acts, and your lack of interest in me and your son. And our life! Where is the old us gone?'

As this brief abusive marriage progressed, Stephen continued to tighten the emotional noose, and being ridiculed, mocked, ignored and insulted became a way of life for Linda.

> Slowly I was being told he wasn't happy with me no matter what I did. He used to say I was always on the go, and to 'chill'. I would look at him and say, 'I have a full-time job, the only permanent one in this household, you don't help with the cleaning or chores, you barely ever pick Jack up from crèche, you don't sort out the bills, or when things have to be paid, or how the money should be spent. I am running the whole household, and looking after Jack. You are never here to do anything with him, so

how can you expect me not to be busy'? When I would ask him to change Jack's nappy he would say, 'Ah you do it please', and give me a sarcastic smile. I would say, 'No! You do it for a change'. But he wouldn't, and I used to end up doing it, or the child wouldn't be changed. When I did leave, the whole single mother thing never really scared me. The way I see it, I have been a single mother to Jack since he was born.

These are samples of a wide range of abusive behaviours designed to control and disempower through emotional means. Abusers, for example, often threaten to leave the victims, and despite being in an abusive situation this threat of abandonment can fill them with fear. Linda, for example, had developed a dependence on Stephen. He sensed this vulnerability, and made this threat:

Stephen would sometimes threaten me with leaving, he would say that he is leaving if something doesn't change – could be anything. That was really scary for me when he would say that – as at the time I could see no existence without him, I wasn't able to see that I would be able to survive financially and emotionally and build a new life for my son and me. He knew I would be scared of this statement. We would often have discussions in the good days, and both of us agreed that we would hate to be single again and looking for someone, as it's hard and lonely.

Some abusers have no hesitation in using their children. I am aware of female abusers denying their ex-partners access to their children. I have talked to victims whose abusers checked their speedometers, and whose phone calls were monitored. Their abusers spied on them when they made or received phone calls, or tried to prevent them from making calls. Some abusers stalk their victims by constantly ringing them to check where they are, and what they are doing. They show excessive jealousy and possessiveness, and frequently call home to make sure that the victim is there. Victims are not permitted time alone, or a space of their own. Children may be used to hurt the victim, by making them spies, or by threatening to call child protection services if the mother threatens to leave the relationship. They are bullied and forced to accept distasteful ideas and behaviours. Their beliefs, gender, sexuality, ability, age and sexual orientation are often ridiculed.

Victims are treated like hostages, and may be denied reminders of their past lives. Their abusive partners may throw out pictures, letters, and mementos of their lives before the relationship. When Linda and Stephen moved into a new house in Newbridge, before he showed his full abusive colours, he laid down the first rule of control:

> . . . that no photos or personal possessions relating to any of my past relationships were to be brought with me, nor were any presents that I may have received from these past relationships. Everything was to be destroyed. So I ended up throwing away photos of past relationships, some of which had good memories. But I did hold onto my debs photos. I put these into the family albums that my mother had, because Stephen would never check these. And I always made sure, if we were ever in my mother's house, that this particular album would never be brought out. Of course, at the time I did wonder why he was so jealous of past relationships as they are in the past and are of no threat to our relationship. But to make him happy I went along with this.

One of my friends, who lived in a remote area, suffered an insidious form of emotional abuse when her abuser was rarely home early, because he worked such long hours. This is a particularly effective and disempowering form of emotional abuse if the victim is a mother without a babysitter for her children. She is tied to the house. The abuser does not have to say anything or forbid anything. He has created a situation of complete control, simply by being absent. He can excuse his behaviour by pointing out how hard he is working to earn 'badly needed' money. He can argue that her job is to mind the children. The rationalisation does not alter the fact that the victim is a housebound hostage subject to his control. This type of emotional abuse creates guilt in the mother who supposes she should not resent being cloistered with her children. Her husband answers to no one. I have also witnessed male victims who were controlled by the 'illnesses' that confined their wives to bed for long periods. The subtle emotional manipulation makes it difficult for these victims to recognise that they are being abused.

Sandra Horley tells one story of vicious emotional abuse, in which a 'charming' husband isolated his wife from family and friends, and then refused to visit her when she was in hospital having their first child. She arrived home to find the word 'slut' traced in the dust on a table. He prevented her from taking a class, and burned all her diaries, drawings and books. When she tried to act independently, he threatened to have her committed to a mental institution.

Though Elaine Weiss's stories describe physical abuse, emotional and verbal abuse is the context of the violence portrayed. One of the narrators spent years in an abusive relationship trying to work out why her husband behaved as he did. She could not understand how anyone could behave is such a way, so she blamed herself. She felt that she must have been provoking him, though she did not know how. In an attempt to appease, she strove always to please him. She believed his taunts and accepted his expectation of perfection from her. The more she strove to be the perfect wife, the more he ridiculed her. He used perfection as a way of controlling her, as she tried to 'get it right'. Because she spent herself on keeping her husband happy, she neglected to meet her own needs and eventually became suicidal.

Emotional abusers are expert in undermining partners in the presence of their children. The victim's authority as a parent is eroded by belittling comments, and she may be blamed for problems with the children, including their behaviour, poor school performance, or even physical defects. In such cases, the children are also abused and shamed. Sometimes this is done in a calm way. This type of emotional abuser never raises his voice, but, with considerable relish, mimics, mocks and derides his victim. She may feel inferior in front of her children, or she may react aggressively, in which case the quiet abuser is perceived as the victim and the angry victim as the abuser.

Victims feel dehumanised and degraded as the perpetrators exploit and isolate them. They are reduced to non-entities when their problems are dismissed, as abusers always put their own needs first. Emotional abusers are adept at instilling guilt in their victims for matters that have nothing to do with them. I have met so many victims who keep asking themselves 'what have I done?' when they are subject to the whims of the abusers, who work in devious ways to control. They may appear kind and caring, making the intended victims feel special, but they gradually spin a web that pulls them in and traps them.

One aspect of emotional abuse rarely mentioned is spiritual abuse. It can occur when victims are prevented from practising their faith, or it may be built into religious tenets that use intolerance and coercion. Many churches exercise control using the tenet of higher purpose; for example, in the context of serving God, they demand tithes of up to 30% of a member's income, and others forbid members to marry outside their church. This can lead to unsuitable marriages, marital breakdown, and a sense of loss because, otherwise, the church member might have found a more compatible partner. I feel that a religiously based decision to forbid specific medical treatments is also spiritual abuse, and may result in loss of life and all the regret that goes with it. Some churches that cling to the notion that they are the only true church may be spiritually abusive, because this belief isolates members, deprives them of external support and, in some cases, of socialising with others. The exclusion of women from playing a full role in a church can also be seen as spiritual abuse, because it denies parity to an entire and equal gender.

More than anything else, I believe that it is emotionally abusive to portray God as a punitive father. Fear is one of the hallmarks of abuse, and negative and forceful preaching that arouses fear in a congregation is spiritual abuse. I think it is also emotionally abusive to ridicule a person's faith. This can be done in a jocular way, but is deeply uncomfortable for the victim. Linda experienced this from an early stage in her relationship.

> One thing, however, that used to bug me during the good part of our relationship was that he used to mock me for my faith. I would pray at night before I go to sleep and he could never understand it – he used say 'there is nothing after this life. What are you praying for? You die and that's the end of you.' But I used to tell him, 'that's your opinion; I believe differently'. However, over time I did leave my faith behind. I guess I was so carried away in my brilliant life that I forgot all about it.

While emotional abuse is prevalent among all classes in society, some sections of the population are more vulnerable. For example, a culture of ageism promotes elder abuse. Elderly people suffer more emotional abuse than any other group. They often face discrimination because of race, disability and infirmity. The old saying 'once a man, twice a child' is a philosophy that effortlessly leads to humiliation. Abusers use emotional blackmail by continuously blaming older people, who become confused and guilty. Their lack of physical strength and diminished mental capacities leave them exposed to abuse. Abusers easily harass them by calling them names, cursing and insulting them, ridiculing them, and threatening to isolate them. They can render them silent by threats of punishment or abandonment. They shout at them and threaten the withdrawal of 'affection', and deny them their rights.

Some of the worst and most widespread types of emotional abuse are directed towards minority groups; for example, gay people are frequent targets for every type of abuse. In the 1950s, extreme homophobia forced some gay people in Britain to try to change their sexual orientation. Some even suffered electric shock treatment to become heterosexual. Only in the 1980s was homosexuality declassified as a mental 'disorder' by psychiatrists. There is little recognition of homosexuality in some countries, where sexuality in general is taboo.

So consistent has been the emotional abuse of homosexuals throughout the ages that some gay people have internalised homophobia, and feel ashamed of their sexual orientation. This deep shame is destructive to self-esteem, identity and close relationships. It leads to distrust and withdrawal from social contact.

Another minority group vulnerable to emotional abuse is people who suffer from disabilities. For example, the refusal of admittance of a physically disabled student to college because of inadequate facilities might be seen as emotional abuse. The victim feels powerless against the institution. Breda Gleeson writes of a case where a person with a disability, who was accompanied by his brother, was refused access to a bus because the driver feared that safety might be jeopardised. The driver had power and the would-be passenger was powerless. It is emotional abuse when suitably qualified employees with disabilities are refused promotion in an organisation. People with disabilities are sometimes given emotionally abusive labels such as 'retard' for cognitive disability, or 'dwarf' for a person of short stature.

Beverly Engel's excellent book *The Emotionally Abusive Relationship* rightly shows that most victims of emotional abuse do not realise they are being abused. They may wonder what is wrong with them as they are constantly criticised for minute aspects of their character. Confused and bewildered, they become full of self-doubt, and may blame themselves for the emotional vacuum in the relationship. Some women feel that if they were 'better 'wives, their husbands would respond to them and love them, but victims do not realise that abusers are unable to give emotional warmth, love or understanding, but are adept at inflicting emotional neglect by withholding approval, appreciation and affection. Instead, they exhibit total indifference. This psychologically devastating combination leads to intense loneliness and frustration, and an erosion of self-confidence and self-esteem.

Victims disintegrate psychologically as the abuser dismantles their emotional and psychological boundaries, in what is akin to brainwashing. Many victims become prisoners in their own homes. For Linda 'it got to the stage in the end that I couldn't even go shopping with a friend, because he would be on the phone asking when I was coming home, because he had some place to go'. Some victims in this state of emotional enslavement experience shame and fear. They become lost in a miasma of insecurity, guilt and anxiety. Hidden emotional scars lead to withdrawal, relationship difficulties and sometimes suicide.

Emotional abuse also has a physiological and behavioural impact leading to depression, sleeping problems, memory loss and body aches. Victims experience a loss of trust, and some suffer from addictions, eating disorders and panic attacks. In their efforts to avoid abuse, victims often alter their thoughts, feelings and behaviours, deny their needs, and some feel that they are going insane.

The negative messages of emotional abuse transfer from generation to generation as abusive communication patterns become the norm, and so I hope this exploration has increased your awareness and enabled you to look at your relationship to ensure that it is abuse-free. There are some pertinent questions you can pose to establish this. Are you are truly happy in your intimate relationship, feeling free to be yourself and having your needs met, or do you feel imprisoned, and have an uneasy feeling bordering on fear? Do you sense that your partner does not wish you well, and resents your success? Are you afforded equality in decision making, and do you feel free to spend money appropriately on your own needs? Are you free to make contact with your family and friends? Do you feel loved, or is your partner warm and attentive at one time, and remote at another? Does he or she humiliate you, and make you feel small in front of others? Are you constantly trying to please your partner and receiving criticism and blame for your efforts?

It might be valuable to write a profile of your relationship. You could begin by labelling it the 'freedom profile'. Imagine your relationship as a garden full of colour and blossoms, gently fluttering in the warm breeze under a cloudless sky. You may, however, have to change it to the 'servitude profile'. Your beautiful garden may only be a plot of weeds and thistles shivering in the cold winter wind. If this is the case, you are courageously acknowledging that you are a victim. If you suffered emotional abandonment and rejection as a child, you may feel unloved and unlovable, so that being in an abusive relationship seemed normal until you realised that your garden is a cold, barren place. Feelings of abandonment indicate a need for counselling. In the safe haven of a counselling room, you can explore your feelings, thoughts, behaviours and spirituality to help resolve those feelings of not being good enough. This is not an easy journey, but I believe that the principal defences against abuse are self-worth and good boundaries, as explored in the early part of this book. You will slowly build and nourish these as you explore your life with your non-judgemental counsellor. The stage will arrive when you will make your decision about staying in an abusive relationship or leaving. This will become clearer in the second last chapter of this book.

Chapter 6

Sexual Abuse

From soul-depth
Suffocated
By invasion-stench.
Nauseated
By skin-smell.
Shamed
By foul-destruction
Of self.
To tear skin off
Reveal bare bones
Scour flesh
To rid the sour taste
Of foul infection
Resting
Within soul.

Jim O'Shea

When I was a teenager in the Ireland of the 1960s, sex was as much on my mind as it is on the minds of teenagers today. But it was a 'dirty' word then. I remember beads of perspiration on my forehead as I knelt in the confessional and admitted to having entertained 'unclean and impure thoughts'. I imagine that this was the experience in many countries at that time, and undoubtedly in earlier decades. The idea of sex being a healthy and loving aspect of our lives was marred. We did not see sex as a loving, giving behaviour, but discussed it furtively as a forbidden and sinful fruit. Our parents informed my friends and me that we were 'found' under 'a head of cabbage', and we knew nothing of the beautiful bond of sexual intercourse between man and woman that gave us life. This life-giving experience is precious. It is mutual, loving and consensual, and, therefore, I am convinced that sexual abuse, which is brutal and loveless, is a severe trauma.

Sexual abusers come from all classes and live 'normal' lives. Their tendencies may be concealed by charming personalities, wealth, professional status, and 'respectability'. Professor Antonia Abbey and her colleagues outline the characteristics of the male sexual abuser hiding behind these masks. He is more hostile towards women than non-abusive men are. He is more likely to hold traditional stereotypes about gender. He takes the victim's power, depersonalises them, and achieves dominance through abusive sexual behaviour.

The abusive personality can be applied as much to sexual abuse as to all other types. The sexual abuser seeks power and control through sexual means, but frequently the sexual abuse is accompanied by verbal, emotional and physical abuse. Sexual abusers see the use of force in relationships as acceptable, and have a strong sense of entitlement to sex. They do not believe that women have a right to say no. They do not admit that forcing a victim to have sex is rape. They perceive sex as a legitimate way to meet their needs, including their sense of satisfaction at bringing their partner to orgasm. They have no respect for their victims, and sex is not an emotionally satisfying experience for them because they see women as sex objects. Watching pornography that portrays the female as ravenous for sex and yearning to please her male partner only confirms this deviant opinion.

Like all abusers, sexual abusers have no concept of boundaries so they invade with impunity. Often their boundaries are sexualised. This situation leads to sexual addictions like pornography, exhibitionism, voyeurism, obscene phone calls, indecent behaviours and serious sexual crimes. Henry Cloud and John Townsend describe this abuser as 'a tyrant, demanding and insatiable'. He may also be a strong consumer of alcohol.

I believe that sexual abusers are more easily able to perpetrate this appalling violence because they do not understand the concept of intimacy. Their feelings are frozen, and this deprives them of pity or comprehending the consequence of violating another person in a very intimate way.

Obtaining statistics to give an accurate picture on sexual abuse is difficult since most studies are about adults who experienced abuse as children. But we can say that sexual abuse is pervasive, and behind these statistics lie innumerable stories of brutality and pain. People of every age, class, race and occupation are targets. Neither tiny infants nor the elderly are exceptions to sexual abuse. The 2002 SAVI (Sexual Abuse and Violence in Ireland) report provides valuable insight into sexual abuse in Ireland. This was a research project carried out by the Health Services Research Centre, Department of Psychology, Royal College of Surgeons in Ireland on behalf of the Dubllin Rape Crisis Centre. This 350-page document shows that 25% of women and 12% of men over 17 years of age experienced adult sexual abuse of some kind. These statistics reflect what is happening globally. It is conservatively estimated that 25% of American women and about 10% of men have been sexually assaulted in adolescence and adulthood. The majority of perpetrators of sexual abuse seem to be male. The abusers of male victims are normally heterosexual. Despite the huge number of victims, sexual abuse is under-reported, and statistics from Canada show that less than 10% of women report sexual assault. Only a tiny percentage of men report it.

It is significant that over 70% of perpetrators are dating partners, friends, authority figures, neighbours, partners, spouses or family friends of the victims. A small number of young adults experience sexual assault from sports coaches.

Many people think that the only type of sexual abuse is rape. But it is far more complex, and includes any form of non-consensual sexual contact or non-touching sexual behaviour. It also encompasses unwanted sexual language or exploitative behaviour. It includes rape, molestation, sexual assault, and any sexual behaviour with someone lacking the mental capacity to consent. Other types of sexual abuse include unwanted touching of genitals or breasts and forced oral, anal or vaginal intrusion. Trying and failing to have sex with an unwilling person is also abuse. Sometimes abusers find 'rough' sex arousing, and enjoy the experience of domination with the rush of power and control it creates, and satisfy their urge to control through aggressive, brutish sexual behaviour.

When the abuser makes decisions about sexual experiences, sexual abuse is taking place. This includes forcing the victim to have sex whenever and however he wishes, making her engage in sex acts with others, or enslaving her into prostitution. Abusers also impose guilt on the victim, making them feel responsible for the abuse. Ironically, they may also withdraw sexual contact in an intimate relationship to abuse and control the victim, whose sexual needs are then unmet. Despite being in sexually abusive relationships, these needs are strong, and I have met many people who complain when their abusive partner rejects them in this way.

Because intimate relations irritate them, sexual abusers are particularly interested in those with whom they have not had sexual relations. Paradoxically, they tend to place women on a pedestal and idealise them. This, however, is simply to ensure protection from real relationships.

The exploitative nature of sexual abuse is seen when perpetrators use people who are unable to make an informed decision, including someone who is asleep, drunk, drugged, disabled, too young, too old, dependent upon or afraid of the perpetrator. The abuser's sense of entitlement incites him to invade a person's boundaries as he wishes.

It is also sexually abusive to mock someone's sexuality or make offensive statements about his/her body. These behaviours also fit the definition of sexual harassment, which is any unwanted sexual behaviour, gesture or comment. Jokes, insults, sexual demands and unwanted attention are also sexual harassment.

The abuser's sexual and power needs, as he envisages them, are all important, and the needs of the victim are side-lined. Sometimes victims are forced to watch pornography as a pretext for learning sexual practices to satisfy the abusers' 'needs'. Abusers sometimes force victims to become involved in pornographic videos for commercial purposes. Some abusers compromise women's sexual health and contraceptive choices by engaging in unsafe sexual practices or insisting the victim undergo an abortion. I have spoken with several young women who unexpectedly found themselves pregnant, and, in a state of confusion, were hurried by their abusers for abortions in England before they could consider their own wishes.

While all sexual abuse is degrading and demoralising, rape is particularly debasing and extremely traumatic. The violence of the assault sometimes immobilises the victims, robbing them of the strength to resist or to flee, as, helpless and terrified, they submit to the torture inflicted on their bodies. In ancient times, this crime incurred more serious penalties than those imposed today. Once, it was a capital crime, and in medieval England the victim was given the option of gouging out the eyes of the perpetrator or of severing his testicles. Long ago, when women were considered chattels, it was perceived as a serious property crime against the man to whom the victim 'belonged'. The female victim was treated as 'damaged goods', and the rapist was forced to pay compensation to her family.

Rape is endemic and global. People who suffer rape come from all age groups and all social backgrounds. It is estimated that almost 200,000 people were raped or sexually assaulted in the US in 2005, and 99% of the perpetrators were male. Only 26% of the perpetrators were strangers. In almost half of the incidents, both the perpetrator and the victim had been drink-ing. Rape is under-reported and under-convicted, and more than 50% of US rapes went unreported to law enforcement. In

2006, 85,000 people were raped in the UK, but only 800 perpetrators were convicted. A similar failure to secure convictions occurs around the world.

There are equally alarming statistics in relation to mass rape. War rape, now recognised as a crime against humanity, goes back to antiquity. However, it has also been a feature of modern conflicts such as the Second World War and other wars. German soldiers raped hundreds of thousands of Russian women following the invasion of Russia, and Soviet troops responded with equally ferocious retaliation against German women towards the end of the war. The Japanese were guilty of mass rape, especially in China, and millions of women were raped during civil wars in Angola, Mozambique, Liberia, Columbia, Guatemala, Rwanda, and so on. Remember, however, that mass rape is as much an act of power and control as any other type of rape. The Germans used it as an act of entitlement and power over a supposedly inferior race, and the Russians retaliated by throwing it into the mix of military power.

The euphemistically titled date rape is also a common experience. Date rape, also called acquaintance rape, is perpetrated not just by dating partners but also by acquaintances, friends or co-workers. Some perpetrators spike the victim's drink with drugs like Rohypnol, Gamma Hydroxy Butyrate, or Ketamine Hydrochloride that act quickly and are almost undetectable. The anaesthetised victim is only vaguely aware of what is happening at the time, and they have no memory of the rape later. Rape is trivialised by the jocose street names of these drugs such as 'Forget-Me-Pill', 'Easy-Lay', 'Scoop Her', 'Ellie', and 'Make-Her-Mine'. Date rape sometimes leads to the unspeakably violent crime of gang rape, which is accompanied by physical assault and humiliation. It causes great distress and powerlessness that can culminate in suicide.

A few of the signs that you may have been raped under the influence of these drugs include soreness or bruising in the genital area, soreness in the anal area, bruising of the thighs, and defensive bruising. You may also experience the side effects of hallucinations, intoxication and feel hung over, with loss of memory for the event. Descriptions from your friends about your behaviour when under the influence of date rape drugs, is a reliable sign of sexual assault. However, only a medical examination, performed before the excretion of the drugs can confirm if you have been drugged.

It is important for you to be aware of this type of rape and to take every precaution to protect yourself when you are socialising. Being with friends and having a charged mobile (cell) phone is strongly recommended. Even more so, it is advisable to remain sober, because alcohol is involved in 50% of sexual assaults. Intoxication exposes victims to sexual predators, who often use the pretext of being drunk as an excuse to commit sexual crimes. Reports in Ireland suggest that Christmas is the worst time for sexual attacks because of the amount of alcohol consumed then. Binge drinking is largely blamed for the increased number of sexual assaults. Inhibitions are lowered by alcohol, but alcohol does not cause or excuse abuse. As I said in the Introduction, an abuser is always an abuser, drunk or sober.

Recent newspaper stories about rape incidents in Ireland reveal that many people have little sympathy for women who are raped when drunk. This attitude is also true of other countries. Research shows that 40% of the public feel that the victim is partly responsible if she has been drinking. Some victims are blamed for their risqué dress or behaviour. Women who wear short skirts and skimpy tops are perceived as 'asking for it'. Women who flirt or dress provocatively do not deserve to be raped, and sexual abusers have little respect for women, regardless of how they dress. In some parts of the world, this disrespect may be part of a culture that sees women as inferior.

Certain segments of the population are more vulnerable to sexual abuse. These include prisoners (male and female), homeless women, disabled women, elderly women and female sex workers (prostitutes).

Prisoners are in a powerless situation, and are often preyed upon by those in power. Many have suffered sexual abuse prior to incarceration. Male prisoners are frequently subject to sexual abuse by criminals, who use their power to terrify them. Females are more likely to suffer abuse at the hands of male prison guards, who, in some countries, have full access to their living quarters. Sexual assault of female prisoners can range from rape to trading sex for privileges. The latter is not consensual, and is an abuse of authority, although many women do not recognise it as such. In the United States, about 25% of female prisoners are sexually abused. If they become pregnant, they have very few maternal rights, and they may even be forced to have an abortion. All states in the US have now made sexual contact between guards and prisoners illegal.

Homeless women, driven to the streets by violent and traumatic lives, often suffer further abuse. They live chaotic and dependent lives, and frequently experience violent and repeated sexual abuse. They rarely report the abuse, partly because they are struggling just to survive. Not only do they lack a home, they have no social support or medical assistance, and endure ill health, addictions and psychological problems. Some resort to prostitution as a means of survival. Poor women with no social support are also at increased risk of rape, as are women of colour who may suffer racist sexual assault.

Research also indicates that disabled people suffer a high level of sexual abuse. It seems that 83% of women with disabilities will be sexually assaulted during their lifetimes. Growing old increases the likelihood of disability, and elderly people in general are vulnerable to sexual abuse. They are powerless and unable to defend themselves. Abusers take advantage of them and have sexual contact with them against their wishes, frequently using force. Apart from sexual acts, sexual abuse of the elderly includes making them observe sex acts, photographing them in sexually explicit ways, showing them pornographic material, spying on them in the bathroom or bedroom, and telling them erotic stories they do not want to hear. Internationally, there are few statistics for sexual abuse of the elderly, but it seems that they are least likely to suffer sexual abuse, as against the other types of abuse.

Family members should be aware of the signs and symptoms of sexual abuse of their elderly relatives. These include being withdrawn, reporting sexual assault, and getting venereal disease or genital infections. Unexplained genital or anal bleeding, torn, stained or bloody underclothing, and bruises around the breasts or genitals are also signs of sexual abuse.

Sex workers are particularly vulnerable targets. They are dehumanised and trafficked like cattle in enormous numbers. For example, it is estimated that up to 16,000 Asian women are trafficked into Canada each year, where they suffer horrendous abuse and exploitation. Studies show that up to 80% of female sex workers suffer rape. There is also a greater incidence of rape in their private lives. Abusive partners' sense of entitlement to do as they wish is heightened with prostituted women, because they seem to think that these women are always available for sex, and that they are 'fair game'. Rape reopens old wounds and traumatic memories of childhood abuse. Studies show that almost 80% of prostituted women have suffered childhood sexual abuse. Unsurprisingly, sex workers rarely report rape. They are also 60–120 times more likely to be murdered than the general public.

Until recently, marital rape or rape by an intimate was widely condoned. Though now illegal, it is still widespread. In the past when women were 'owned', it was expected and accepted that the male partner was entitled to have sex whenever he wanted it, regardless of his partner's feelings. Now it is recognised that marital rape is domestic violence in its worst form. It is rarely an isolated occurrence, but happens frequently in the relationship, and the victims begin to question if they are condoning it by staying in the abusive relationship. Some women put up with marital rape in the hope that it might elicit the loving, caring side shown by their partners before marriage.

Marital rape can take several forms. It may be violent, or abusers may use it as a form of 'making up' after a bout of physical or emotional abuse. Such 'making up' is a clear reflection of how far the abuser is from understanding the meaning of love or intimacy. Domination can also mean holding the partner in one position so that she cannot move during the sex act, or it may be sadistic where the victim is coerced into acts which degrade and humiliate her. The abuser may say that he wants sex as proof of his partner's love for him. He equates attachment with love, and fails to see that having sex is not always a loving experience.

All abuse has a damaging impact on victims. The type, extent and duration of the abuse are some of the factors that determine the level of suffering endured by the victim. I believe that sexual abuse, which breaches the most personal and sacred boundaries, has the greatest impact of all, and much of it is long term. Rape leaves severe psychological and emotional scars on the victim, and it may take years before it is disclosed. Men, for example, who have been raped as adults may never disclose. They find it so shameful that they dull their pain with alcohol or drugs, or perhaps commit suicide. Rape can lead to post traumatic stress, extreme fear, rage, and panic attacks. Victims may develop eating disorders, have nightmares, and experience suicidal thoughts and behaviours. In their revulsion at being sexually degraded, they sometimes wash compulsively and self-harm. Many experience relationship difficulties and are fearful of expressing intimacy. They feel humiliated, defiled, worthless and guilty. It is little wonder that they find it difficult to trust, and sometimes withdraw from social contact. I have met victims who suffer from depression and somatic ailments, and find it difficult to perform normal tasks.

Marital rape causes as much trauma as rape by a stranger. This violent act can inflict physical injuries to sexual areas, as well as emotional and psychological damage, leading to fear, depression, anger and anxiety. It can lead to long-term consequences such as eating disorders, depression, fear of sex, lack of sexual enjoyment, and sleeping problems. Rape by a spouse breaks a deep trust, and causes the victim to question her value as a lovable individual. It betrays the fundamental basis of the marital relationship and shatters every understanding victims have, not only of their partners and the marriage, but also of themselves. Women sometimes question if what is happening is really rape.

The violence of rape should not blind us to the fact that all sexual abuse has serious consequences. Victims, for example, who have been inappropriately fondled experience many of the same feelings as rape victims. It is vitally important for friends, family and therapists not to minimise any form of sexual abuse.

I believe that therapy offers the best option to deal with these damaging effects. Rape crisis centres are, in my opinion, excellently positioned to deal with this trauma. Many victims are unwilling to go to the police following sexual assault. You should, however, be aware that many countries have special units in hospitals to deal with this trauma. In Ireland, these are known as Sexual Assault Treatment Units. Currently, they are located in Dublin (Rotunda), Waterford (Regional), Cork (South Infirmary Victoria University), Mullingar (Midlands Regional), Galway (Hazelwood House) and Donegal (Letterkenny). They cater for male and female victims of 14 years upwards. It is a free and confidential service, and can be accessed through the police, GP, Rape Crisis Centres, or by self-referral. There are no time limitations for attending, and victims can attend without police involvement, if they wish. The website of the Cork South Infirmary Victoria University Hospital is informative about the excellent services these units provide.

Ultimately, victims have to integrate it like any trauma, and then they can lead fulfilled and happy lives. There are many people who have recovered from rape through appropriate therapy and went on to form happy, healthy relationships with non-abusive partners. The love and support of family and friends combined with counselling is a powerful antidote to the suffering that comes from sexual abuse.

Chapter 7

Financial Abuse

I am lost.
Deserted in my loneliness.
I gave so much
In my time,
Love, nurture, protection, succour.
I am lost.
The years are gone,
Slipped slowly on,
Written in the lines on my face,
In the faded blue of my eyes,
In the stumble of my gait,
In the trembling of my hands.
I am lost.

Jim O'Shea

We return to Linda's story here. Not only was she physically, emotionally and verbally abused, but she also suffered severe financial abuse, which has serious implications for her credit rating, and her ability to borrow in the future.

In the early days when Stephen's moods began to darken, she felt pressurised to part with her beloved car to satisfy his selfish desire, for what she saw as his 'happiness'.

I once had a car I loved – my BMW – I had worked hard to get this car, and paid off the loan. One weekend my husband and I drove to Belfast to look at a car that he adored and wanted. Finances, however, were not going to stretch for this car. The garage owner said to him that they would consider my car as a trade in, as they liked it, so he would only have to put a small balance to it. At first, I said 'no way'. But on our journey home he became so depressed and was in such a bad mood. I knew this was going to last. He was blaming me for not being able to get the car, and said that the power was in my hands to get his dream car, and he said that cars didn't mean as much to me as to him. He kept telling me that this could be 'our car'. This went on for days and in the end I gave in. Life was too short to live like this over a car. Yes, I did like my car, but Stephen's happiness was more important, and if he was going to get so depressed over it I would just agree to the trade in, and we could get back to normal. So the following week we went back to the garage and made the swap. I was sad at the loss of my car, but I knew that there were more important things in life. Stephen's happiness used to give me such a kick!

As Stephen's abusive nature became fully evident, Linda goes on to reveal how she was practically impoverished by his profligacy and irresponsibility. He often spent his weekly wages on alcohol, and she was forced to pay the mortgage and bills from her own income. She was, she said, 'walking on eggshells to try and please him', as he blithely ignored the bills, some of which were due to his overspending. When she protested and asked him to look at a bill, he would continue to watch television and 'tell me that I was good at those sort of things and hand it back to me – worry and all'. The situation deteriorated as Stephen started businesses that failed as he lost interest in them, and 'life began to become one big mess of debts and bills'. He became angry when there were insufficient funds for him to indulge himself with new parts for his car, and blamed his hardworking wife, who managed the money with remarkable expertise. However, she could not cope as his extravagance and irresponsibility increased.

He began to take the chequebook, write out cheques to cash, and cash them to get what he wanted. Of course, he would spend the money, and only then tell me about it.

> He used to assure me not to worry that he would have the money for the account in a week or so. I often believed him, and gave him the benefit of the doubt. But he never stuck to his word. This would mean that I would have to re-jig our money, or go short on something to cover bills. In the end, I had to start hiding the chequebooks and credit cards because he just didn't get it. It became my problem, because if I didn't sort it out cheques would bounce.

Not only did he place all the responsibility on her shoulders, but, as is the way with abusive people, he also mocked her. His sense of entitlement knew few bounds, and reached a new height about three weeks before Christmas one year when

> ... he came home with a new van for which he had signed finance for €15,000. I looked at him drive it in. He had a smile from ear to ear. I just couldn't believe it. I was so mad at him. We couldn't afford this. He hadn't even discussed this with me. It was a huge amount of money to spend without mentioning to your wife, especially when we were really struggling with the monthly finance payments. But, once again, he said he had a new business deal coming up, and not to worry, that it would be easy to pay for the van. Once again, an empty promise – and guess who was left dealing with the monthly payments?

The abusive mindset does not change without significant therapeutic intervention, and matters did not improve when Linda left. He continued to live in the family home while she rented a house near her parents. Despite living there, he refused to contribute to the mortgage, and she had to bring him to court for maintenance money. He treated the court agreements with the same disdain as he treated Linda and their child. He emigrated to Canada, owing her thousands of euro maintenance, and to this day she continues her struggle to pay mortgage and bills.

The pinnacle of his abuse became apparent when she repossessed the house following his departure.

One day he posted the key to our family home to me, so I presumed he had moved out. I had been asking him to do this for a while. So I could rent it and start paying the mortgage. I went up to the house and what I found was a shell. Everything was gone – all the family possessions – gone! Cooker, washing machine, dishwasher, furniture, couches, TV unit, conservatory furniture, beds. Everything that was in the house was gone. He had even unscrewed the curtain poles and the tieback holders for the curtains and taken them, as well as the curtains. He took the drive-on lawnmower, the garden furniture, and everything that was in the shed. He even took the shed.

He took the flower pots, but left the clay and flowers. He also took the oil tank. All that was left were things that couldn't be taken because they were part of the house like the kitchen presses and the bath, toilet and shower. Everything else was gone! I was gutted! Totally gutted! This was spite as well as greed. Who needs tieback holders for curtains? These items were half mine, and Jack had a right to them as well. Now they are gone, and so was he. He had taken off, and was freeing himself of all these burdens. I was left with every single debt, a child to raise, a house that was cleared out that I couldn't rent, because I didn't have the funds to refurbish it. I couldn't exactly ring the gardaí and tell them I was robbed because in criminal law I wasn't robbed because he owned these things as well. Of course, in the family law sense this is very much wrong. According to family law, it is unlawful to remove family chattels until the assets are split in separation.

This was not, as Linda supposed, either spite or greed. It was control, and a desire to humiliate. It was a sense of entitlement and extreme disrespect. As he fled from his wife and child, Stephen's actions spoke eloquently about how he felt about them.

The empty house was filthy, with rubbish everywhere – bottles and cigarettes inside and outside the house, and rubbish bags everywhere. He had left me with nothing; I didn't even have a good car, because he had sold his precious car, and had crashed my car a few days before I left. So I bought a car worth about one thousand euro to get around, and had to cope with a mortgage and bills, and platefuls of worry! I felt really hard done by. He had just gone to another country to start fresh with no bills or responsibilities, while I was left to pick up the pieces of this mess.

Linda's story contains some elements of financial abuse, which is the misappropriation of victims' resources, or denying them sufficient money through various means. This abuse is found in all social groups. It is perpetrated in personal and professional relationships and on vulnerable people, when power, control, and dominance are exercised through money. It involves isolating victims in order to control and exploit their finances. By isolating them from their families and friends, abusers can do this without interference, and use their property, finances or assets exclusively for their own benefit, or for improper purposes. Even when someone has legitimate access to another's assets, financial abuse can occur through misuse of finances or failing to meet the victim's material needs. Withholding finances for the bare necessities of life is seriously abusive. Financial abuse occurs in the workplace, when an employee is wrongly denied a promotion, sacked without good reason, or overworked without remuneration.

In intimate relationships, financial abusers use many controlling tactics to create a hellish life for their victims. They create dependency by forbidding their victims to work. Homemakers, usually women, are particularly vulnerable to financial abuse. I met one victim whose husband wordlessly left the housekeeping money on the mantelpiece each week. She was not allowed to have a banking card. She had to account for every penny. Some abusers resort to weighing the fruit their wives purchase to control their expenditure. Victims are denigrated, and told that they have no right to the family income. They are forced to ask, even beg, for money to run the house. Even then, they may be denied sufficient funds. Victims do not receive any recognition of their value as homemakers. Imagine what it would cost to bring in a person to run a house full time for seven days a week. Just consider what it costs working couples for childminding facilities for five days.

If both partners work, the abuser may demand a partner's pay cheque at the end of the week and deny him/her responsibility in financial decisions. Financial abusers may also put all of the family bills in the victim's name, but conceal banking records, bills or credit records. Some abusers confiscate social welfare grants and children's allowance for themselves, and others force their partners to work and carry all the financial responsibility of the house, but then mishandle and squander the money. This is exactly what happened to Linda, who valiantly struggled to survive a mountain of unpaid debts, and cope with the cruel disregard and disrespect of her husband, who fled from his obligations.

Financial abuse is often inflicted on vulnerable people who have diminished capacity to manage their affairs and on those who are at risk of financial manipulation, including people living alone, divorced or separated, and those with disabilities. The elderly, especially those who have accumulated wealth, are very vulnerable. In 2006, children of the elderly in Britain stole almost £3 million from their parents. The rate of frauds on older people is enormous, with only a minute percentage reported. Detective Joe Roubicek investigated more than 1,000 cases of financial fraud and exploitation of elderly Americans, and outlines some of these in his book *Financial Abuse of the Elderly*. Little wonder that financial abuse of the elderly is labelled the crime of the twenty-first century.

It can be as simple as taking money from a person's purse, and continuous theft of money in this way can result in destitution. Some years ago, I became aware that my mother's pension was being stolen every week. She was over 80 and living alone. The abuse began with a few euro, and finally escalated to the theft of her entire pension. I noticed that something was wrong when my 'pocket money' of 5 euro per week was reduced to 5 cents. I became worried and searched her handbag to discover that she only had a few cents. Eventually, I took over the collection of her pension.

Financial abuse is usually perpetrated by people the victim trusts, including relatives, carers, friends and neighbours. Joe Roubicek outlines one case study where a carer took tens of thousands of dollars from an elderly couple. Remarkably, because they liked and relied on the abuser, they refused to press charges.

Roubicek's case studies show how simple it is for abusers to persuade the elderly to give them control of their money. It is not unusual for elderly people to allow carers or favourite relatives the use of their credit or ATM card, and familiar predators can easily persuade elderly relatives for permission to use their names to get credit. Some abusers take advantage of old people by moving into their homes on the pretext that they will look after them and keep them company. Once ensconced, they pressure them to give gifts, trick them into paying for work that is never done, or persuade them to invest in bogus business opportunities or lottery swindles.

As in my mother's case, abusers are cautious initially, and confine themselves to stealing a small amount of money or jewellery before moving on to more blatant and even violent abuse. Violent abuse includes forcing the elderly into selling their homes, or threatening to kick them out and render them destitute. Financial abusers work in secret. Abusive relatives or carers keep their victims in the dark about their financial situation, and withhold information about welfare benefits. Part of this deception can include forging signatures on pension cheques and legal papers like wills, or misusing power of attorney.

People with Alzheimer's or dementia, those taking heavy medication or those who suffer from memory loss and mental disorientation are easy targets. They simply cannot remember what happened when defrauded and are unable to distinguish between one document and another. They will generally sign anything put in front of them. These victims are manipulated to put their abusers' names on bank accounts, giving them access to considerable wealth, which ultimately bankrupts them.

The elderly should be aware of the many scams fabricated to part them from their money. Mail scams are particularly powerful. Lottery and sweepstake letters emblazoned with the person's name tell them that they have won an enormous amount of money. Of course, a purchase is necessary to avail of the attractive prize! Sometimes fake cheques are included to make the fraud more personal and attractive.

Computer scams leading to identity theft are particularly difficult to recognise. The scammers are looking for as much personal information as possible to help them steal a person's identity, and gain access to bank accounts and credit cards. Identity theft is increasing at a significant rate in the US, with more than 500,000 cases each year. Pension book numbers, credit card numbers, driver's licence numbers, telephone numbers, social security numbers and medical card numbers are used to unlock caches of money or goods. Account numbers for telephone, electricity or gas bills are valuable to scammers.

On a daily basis, I get emails from sham webmail companies about so-called congestion 'due to anonymous registration of webmail accounts'. They threaten to suspend my email account unless I send my username, password, date of birth and resident country. I immediately delete them. But others are very convincing. Sometimes, when entering a website or downloading a piece of information, you are asked to sign on, and give your email address and password. You may comply from force of habit, and unwittingly give someone the means of accessing your email account. This enables them to get further information such as bank details.

Recently I received a sham email, supposedly from my bank, sporting the bank's logo, that convinced me to click on the link provided. This simple click exposed me to the Trojan virus, which remains hidden in computer systems and passes on passwords and codes to a remote computer, often in a distant country. Remember that banks never ask you to respond by email or to click onto a website. Many people fall into this devious trap. Users should consider protecting their computers with anti-viral software. Con artists also target elderly people through telemarketing fraud and predatory lending. They generally try to confuse the elderly into parting with their money for 'worthwhile and once-off offers'. They try to complete the fraud quickly, before the elderly person can consult with relatives.

Home improvement scams requiring significant expenditure are also quite common. Fraudsters present themselves as well-educated, caring individuals. They are well dressed, suave and persuasive. They build up a relationship quickly with the elderly victims to gain their trust. They present themselves as experts, use first names, and tell their victims that they have been in the area doing some work. They promise to do the work cheaply. The abusers are experts in persuading elderly people that their house needs repair, but then they do shoddy and incomplete work. Joe Roubicek's stories show that some victims are so mentally impaired they fail to remember signing cheques for so-called home improvements. Elderly women living alone are prime targets for these abusers, because they are often lonely and unaware of being duped and swindled.

Families may be unaware that their elderly members are suffering financial abuse. Despite visiting my mother every week for years, I had no idea that she was becoming destitute. When I discovered that she had no money in her handbag, I assumed that she was concealing her money somewhere in the house. At that stage, her mental powers were failing. Eventually someone told me what was happening.

We may not think that it can happen to us, so it is important to be aware of potential financial abuse of our elderly relatives, especially if they are failing mentally. We must visit them regularly and actively protect them. We may notice unpaid bills or the disappearance of valuable possessions. We can get their permission to check their bank accounts for withdrawal of large sums of money. We can examine signatures on cheques or other papers that look suspicious, or find out why additional names appear on their accounts or credit cards. We may have to investigate why bank statements are no longer being sent to the older person's home, or discover who is withdrawing money from ATMs, when the elderly person cannot get to the bank. If we notice that a second mortgage has been taken out in the elderly person's name, or if there has been a change in financial routines, we should investigate. We might notice sudden changes in a will or financial document. Constant contact through visits and telephone calls can protect our elderly relatives.

Unnecessary home repairs or physical changes in our elderly family members are obvious signs of subversive abuse. We may notice they are becoming unkempt or their hygiene has deteriorated. We should pay attention to changes in their behaviour such as fear, shame or depression, or other signs such as confusion, anger, helplessness and secretiveness. Older adults who have not lost the power of rational thinking can take certain measures to prevent financial abuse. They can join social groups and stay in constant contact with trusted relatives. They should deposit money in a bank rather than conceal it in their home. Reliable family members can hold valuable documents, and examine papers elderly relatives are asked to sign. Older people can also look to their lawyer, their clergyman, and social services for advice and support. Above all, it is important to anticipate the time when they may become utterly vulnerable as they enter very old age, by arranging for trusted relatives to help them when they need to withdraw money or collect their pension.

It is easy to minimise financial abuse because it is subversive, but its consequences are as devastating and disempowering as any other type of abuse. It displays the same disrespect for our boundaries as other abuses, because fraudsters steal the fruits of our labours. It is also as personal, because our finances are an intimate part of our lives necessary for our subsistence and enjoyment, and they are appropriated by someone else, who, more than likely, has a poor work ethic. It has the added dimension of possibly impoverishing us, stressing us, and preventing us from enjoying life as much as we might desire.

Chapter 8

Abuse in the Workplace and in School

Shames spirit,
Power infected,
Poisonous intent,
No happiness found there,
Only spiritual starvation.
Humanity shrivelled.
Powerless to protest,
A futile rebellion
Against cruel oppression,
Unspoken,
Looks that can kill,
Scowls of derision,
An abyss of degradation,
Imprisoning sense of self.

Jim O'Shea

As she explored her painful experiences of severe workplace bullying, Anna, one of my clients, set about reclaiming her power by writing an 'unsent letter' to her ex-boss, Mark. Anna is well qualified, and has a university degree, but Mark was so abusive that she eventually had to leave work, and she angrily told me how the company had accepted her letter of 'resignation' and wished her well for the future. Her letter will give you an insight into the nature of workplace bullying, and how destructive it is to unsuspecting victims.

Mark,
Ever since I left my job, which you forced me to do, I have been through hell, all because of you and how you

97

treated me for the past year. Every day I was afraid to go to work and was sick every morning at the thoughts of it, and you, and your behaviour. You treated me like dirt.

It was the same every day. Not even a hello from you in the mornings, constant shouting and roaring at me, blaming me for everything and making little of me in front of the others. It got to the stage that I was nearly physically sick most days because of this, and more. Not being able to leave my desk without you ringing to see where I was, not being able to go to the bathroom without permission, because you, or no one else, had the sense or the decency to answer the phone. It felt so degrading to have to ask permission to go to the toilet.

The atmosphere in the office was awful in the last few months I was there, mainly because of you. Expecting me to do absolutely everything for you, and yet not letting me leave my desk to do other parts of my job. Do you know how that feels to be almost followed everywhere you go and to fear leaving your desk because I'd get given out to? No! You don't, because no one tells you what to do.

I hate the way you tell everyone what to do, even people that don't work there. You just love being in control of everything or you fly off the handle. You're weak, that's why. Almost paranoid at times when you don't know exactly what's going on.

You made my life a misery. I couldn't get you or work out of my head, even at weekends, because of the fear I felt. The fear of you and what you'd say next or blame me for next. I felt I could do nothing right, you made me feel stupid, bad at my job, because everything I did was someway wrong, mainly because I wasn't Margaret or I didn't do it her way. Since she came back from America, you started treating me 100 times worse than you used to. Shouting at me every morning, blaming me for things that had nothing to do with me, taking all your anger out on me and making me feel guilty for being out sick. The morning I left you even dared me to count how many sick days I had last year.

That morning you were so horrible to me. I really wanted to sort things out, discuss it properly, but you just treated me like dirt. I'll never forget the way you spoke to me. You didn't even say thank you for all my work or sorry for what you did. You just wanted Margaret back, and that was it, never mind about me.

I just want you to know how sick I was when I left, and that it's only now, nearly two months later, that I'm starting to feel myself again. I used to be afraid to do anything because I had so little confidence in myself. All because of how your treated me. You wouldn't ever let me do any other work, only answer the phones and other 'dogs' work that no one else had the time to do. I was a fool, too soft, and you really took advantage of that. The pity of it is that I was so proud to work there at the start. I even told people to go to your company to get work done, and what thanks did I ever get only abuse. You never trusted me to do any sort of challenging work, and I started to believe I was useless, that I could do nothing only answer phones. You made me feel so worthless and not just at work. You wouldn't even let me go home early when the snow was very bad; you just gave out to me again. I hated you so much from then on. Since January it was like you upped your bullying game against me to force me out. It got so bad, you made my life miserable and you didn't even care. All you care about is money, and competing with your friend's company.

Well, Mark, I want you to know that I'm over all that now and getting my life back on track. I don't need you or your stupid job anymore. I've never been happier. I don't care about you and I am going to be happier and more successful than you'll ever be. You'll end up a very sad and lonely man if you keep treating people the way you treated me.

That was a more serious case of bullying than the racist bullying that I experienced in the 1960s, when I was 19 years old, and working in another country. I was hardworking, but shy. A rural child who had seen little of life or of the world.

Perhaps a target for bullying! Most of my colleagues were kind and helpful. I think, however, that one elderly man did not have a favourable view of Irish people. Sometimes I worked for him in the evening, and found that he did not properly explain my tasks. I struggled to comply with his instructions, and soon began to feel his irritation, when he turned on me with the words 'stupid Paddy. How can you be so stupid! I've explained this to you, and it's so simple. Stupid Paddy.'

These examples contain some behaviours at the heart of workplace bullying, which Susan Harthill defines as 'repeated offensive behaviour through vindictive, cruel, malicious or humiliating attempts to undermine an individual or group of employees'. It is often based on sex, race, age, marital or family status, religion, disability, sexual orientation and nationality. Perpetrators exert control by marginalising and demeaning their victims. Targets include new employees or workers who are better qualified, more efficient, or more popular than the abusers. They become jealous of a subordinate's or co-worker's exceptional skills. Envy enflames the abuser's sense of inadequacy, especially if the victim refuses to be subservient. My opinion, however, is that becoming subservient only encourages the cowardly bully to increase his controlling, abusive behaviour. The abuser might resent the professional qualifications or social skills of the victim. Just as abusers feel uncomfortable in intimate situations, workplace abusers constantly feel irritated and angry in their professional relationships with their victims.

It is important to recognise the wide variety of abusive behaviours in the workplace. They range from verbal, emotional, physical and sexual to financial, all designed to exert power and control. Emotional bullying is the hardest to prove, which is why it is likely to be the most common. It is closely allied to verbal bullying. The entire process undermines a person, by intimidation and slander, or by giving one person's work to another. Boycotting, isolation, sarcasm, whispering about a person in their presence, and making loud negative comments about their 'incompetence' are all part of the abuser's tactics. Spying, deceit and stalking may accompany these behaviours. Perpetrators glare, they are rude, they scream, and they use threats of violence to render their victims helpless. Sexual abuse includes unwanted touching, fondling, kissing, lewd and sexual remarks or jokes. These actions may culminate in sexual assault and rape.

Workplace bullying is global, and like domestic abuse it is greatly under-reported. Females are more likely to be bullied than men, although both men and women are equally likely to be bullies. Statistics vary greatly in different countries and in different careers. Statistics reported from the US are disturbing. At least 23 million workers are subject to bullying during their working lives, and the poison it engenders affects millions of families. A Dublin-based study suggests that 5% of workers in the EU endure bullying. It appears that health, social work, education, public administration and transport are the most affected sectors. Studies in Finland show that workplace bullying, especially for women, has increased significantly since the 1990s. Unfortunately, as Margaret Kohut reveals in her book *Understanding, Controlling, and Stopping Bullies & Bullying at Work*, many victims eventually lose or leave their jobs.

Bullying wreaks havoc on how a company operates. It creates low morale, depression, tension, reduced efficiency, a high number of court cases, and a high rate of absenteeism. In 2005, UK businesses lost 18 million working days because of bullying. Absenteeism and lost productivity due to workplace harassment cost more than €100 million in the British health service alone.

And who are the people who cause such distress? They are the same people who can cause misery in intimate relationships, because workplace bullying is similar in many respects to domestic abuse. Therefore, understanding the abusive personality type and the organisational ethos of a company helps to explain workplace bullying. Margaret Kohut paints a portrait of bullies based on personality disorders that offers a valuable approach to understanding them. As with domestic abusers, workplace abusers may have a Jekyll and Hyde personality – vicious and vindictive in private yet charming in front of others. Workplace abusers are shallow, articulate, dishonourable and poisonous. These cowards are impulsive, irresponsible and attention seeking. They fawn before superiors, behave inappropriately with colleagues, and exploit the weaknesses and vulnerability of others. They are mean-spirited, devious and manipulative. They lack generosity, taking all the credit for workplace performance. They single people out, show favouritism, and co-opt henchmen. They devalue, disrespect and exclude others. Their arrogance and insecurity demand domination. Workplace bullies have a low level of sensitivity and poor interpersonal skills. They care only about themselves and are intolerant of others. Like domestic abusers, they are divisive, dictatorial and dishonest. They are predators who take pleasure from exerting power over others.

Managers and supervisors account for 80% of bullying, which manifests as shouting or insulting subordinates. However, bosses can be bullied too. Having authority does not always mean having the power to match. For example, research in Ireland shows that a significant number of primary school principals are victims of bullying by staff members. Some managers depend on their subordinates for expertise, and an abusive subordinate can subtly withhold it. The abusive subordinate can also stay away from meetings, or make excuses to leave the workplace, pretending that they are unwell, while they backbite and undermine their superiors. They are adept at using moral blackmail and at fomenting resistance to change in the workplace. Managers and supervisors are reluctant to seek help because they fear that it might damage their authority. They do not understand that the abusive personality type has no respect for authority, or for appropriate boundaries.

Since abuse is based on power and control, bullying is easily facilitated in hierarchical organisations such as the army or the police, which are based on military obedience and power. Such 'official' power can breed the worst cases of abuse and generate utter helplessness in the victim. General Haig ordered the execution of over 300 soldiers during the First World War to inspire fear in the remaining soldiers. Research shows evidence of rampant bullying in police and military forces around the world. It is accompanied by persistent denial or minimisation of bullying by upper management.

The power exercised by upper management in the police was seen in Ireland in 2009, when the police threatened to strike following wage cutbacks during the economic crisis. They were immediately threatened with arrest and imprisonment if they proceeded with strike. This view is understandable in the context of the security of the state, but the threat shows that the naked power of management needs to be exercised with responsibility.

There is plenty of scope for intimidation, threats of legal action, and muzzling in these hierarchical organisations. Employees may be denied promotion, demoted, or shifted throughout the organisation without consultation. Their contracts may be terminated without good reason.

Bullying by individuals is very damaging, but mob bullying can bring increased trauma. Margaret Kohut reveals how she was mob bullied within the US armed forces. Mobbing is a collective campaign by co-workers to exclude, punish and humiliate a worker to push them out of an organisation. This widespread behaviour is extremely detrimental, because the victim is utterly isolated and demoralised. Margaret Kohut refers to it as emotional assault. Mobbing is even more destructive when management sides with the abusers and perceives the victim as the problem.

However, bullying exists in all organisations and affects every type of worker, although it is particularly widespread among professionals. It can be especially prevalent in businesses trying to survive fierce global competition. Enormous pressure and unreasonable demands are placed on employees. This is the age of productivity where companies are made 'lean', a euphemism for eliminating surplus employees. Ambitious targets are set. When they are met, they are raised. This cycle creates stress and ultimately failure for the struggling employee. When a person is branded a failure for falling short of targets, it is an attack on the self. This kind of attack intensifies if unwarranted poor performance reports are part of the mix.

Such a message conveys an image of worthlessness, breeds low self-esteem, and creates irrational guilt, which affects people's quality of life. Managers are subject to the same pressure, and their heads are always on the block in the mad rush for profits and survival. This hierarchical treadmill may develop into corporate bullying, which is subtly different to institutional or endemic bullying, which is part of the organisation's ethos. Corporate bullying can include forcing employees to work excessive hours, sacking ill employees, searching a worker's files, listening to private conversations, giving poor reports, and generally pressuring workers. In this environment, the bully acts with impunity.

Economic recessions encourage an abusive national outlook. Listening to commentators and callers on the national airwaves in Ireland during the savage downturn, which began in 2009, is disturbing. One participant had a very specific 'cure', when discussing productivity and efficiency in the public service on the television programme 'Questions and Answers'. He angrily proclaimed that any inefficient public service worker should be sacked. This person, ignoring the fact that inefficiency in the public service has more to do with the system than the individual, was advocating the abuse of power to deprive a family of the means to live, without exploring non-abusive and non-power-based ways of increasing productivity. He was advocating financial abuse. Recently, I was disgusted at the statement of a spokesman for the rating agency Fitch who was concerned at the low rate of house repossessions in Ireland. Abuse has no humanity, and this statement sidelined the human suffering involved in losing one's house. It reminded me of the Establishment during the Famine, who secretly rejoiced at the eviction rate and the prospect of larger farms, when the unfortunate tenants had left for America.

Recently, electronic or cyber bullying has become wide-spread. Abusers use mobile phones, email, websites, Facebook and so on. Cyber bullying exerts powerful control over others. Its anonymity gives the abuser *carte blanche*. Bullies stalk their colleagues in cyberspace, where they can conceal their own identities and their own lack of self-esteem. Women seem to be the main targets of cyber bullying, which includes ridiculing comments, making threats, sexual remarks, disclosing their private information, or hacking into their computers. Websites can be specifically created to humiliate and demean people.

The consequences of workplace bullying are horrific. In the course of my counselling work, I am always disturbed at the acute stress and demoralisation workplace victims endure. They suffer physically, mentally and financially. Their behaviour changes as they sink into anxiety and depression. As in Anna's case, the bully's image and voice is constantly in the victim's mind, so that many find it difficult to sleep, relax or work. Monday mornings are a nightmare for them. They alternate between anger and helplessness. They feel isolated, shamed and guilty as they struggle to survive in a toxic and exhausting workplace. Some abuse drugs and drink to avoid the pain and hurt they feel. Victims of long-term bullying manifest symptoms of Post Traumatic Stress Disorder, panic attacks, and suicidal thoughts.

Victims of workplace abuse also experience many physical and psychosomatic complaints, including skin problems, heart palpitations, migraine, dizziness, headaches and gastric complaints. Their immune system is adversely affected. Some get high blood pressure. They lose concentration, suffer accidents,

e difficult to live with as their focus is entirely
ɔm family life to work. The victim's partner has to
ch his/her mood swings, as well as suffering the
nic consequences of bullying. When victims take time off
wᴄ ᴄ, they must rely on social welfare payments. Sometimes
they simply resign to escape the torment.

As the bullying and controlling intensifies, the victims' self-confidence diminishes. They lose perspective and doubt their ability to do their work. They undervalue their opinions and ideas and, more importantly, their worth, as they are isolated and undermined. They experience loss of control, helplessness and fear as they bend to another's will. Victims may withdraw from society and even from their families.

There is a responsibility on employers and employees alike to confront workplace abuse. Targets should confront it in the early stages before they fall prey to these pernicious consequences. A plan for confronting and surviving workplace bullies includes replacing negative self-talk with positive affirmations, and accessing the network of support provided by friends, family, therapists, doctors, lawyers, trade unions, newspaper reporters and internet organisations that target bullying. Even with anti-bullying policies and structures, which should always be used, it is not easy to confront the cunning and arrogant abusive personality type. Bullies are not amenable to persuasion. They often have a support network of their own. Sometimes the abuse gets worse when it is reported, but it is still vital to confront it. As with domestic violence, it will get worse anyway. When confronting the abuser, endeavour to always remain calm, conceal fear, stick to the facts, and use non-aggressive language. State your feelings about such maltreatment, but try not to allow the abuser to see your vulnerability, or he/she will exploit it.

If you are unable to face the abuser, put your complaint in writing, and use a friend or therapist for feedback to ensure that your memo is effective. Mediation is also an option. There are professional mediators and consultants who specialise in resolving bullying. Brendan Schutte's book *Fixing the Fighting: a guide to using mediation in settling disputes and resolving conflict in the workplace* elaborates on this process. Generally, it is better to confront the abuse from within rather than going public. Whistleblowers must be prepared for 'dirty' counter-measures by the organisation

Keeping an anecdotal record of the abusive encounters is essential. Since emotional and psychological abuse is difficult to define and prove, they may appear trivial unless written down. Useful anecdotal records show a pattern of bullying. Isolated incidents are not considered bullying. The diary should record the date, time and place of each episode. It should describe the effect the event had on the victim, whether medical help was sought, and how it affected the victim's ability to do her job. It should also include incidents where the abuser has not followed company rules or procedures. However, be prepared for a response, which may blame your symptoms on something else. Organisations are reluctant to accept responsibility for the psychological complaints of a worker, which is why so many do not complain about work-place bullying. If you decide to go for counselling, this can be turned against you. You are then the one with the problem! You are the one who is mentally unstable, and needs help! On the other hand, it can bring employers to heel if they feel that an accusation of causing stress, necessitating therapy, might be made against them.

If the organisation is unionised, alert the union, which may provide a sufficient buffer to persuade the bully to back off. The union will also help you understand the company's complaints procedure. If there is no union, Human Resources will help. In some countries, there is also an external source of appeal, such as the Rights Commissioner in Ireland.

Governments all over the world have passed anti-bullying legislation, with varying degrees of success. However, legisla-tion will not change the abusive personality type, and it will not lower company expectation of high profits or peak performances. It is important that you acquaint yourself with the legislation of your country. Counsellors, unions, government agencies, human resource departments, mediators and lawyers can clarify the process. Legislation on workplace abuse is too complex to deal with here, but it is often enshrined in labour laws, equality laws, health and safety laws, and disability legislation. Every country has its own legislative or quasi-legislative approaches. The barrister John Eardly provides useful insight into Irish legislation in his book *Bullying and Stress in the Workplace: employers and employees – a guide.*

If the bullying persists after using informal, formal and external procedures, consider the last resort of leaving the abusive workplace. In times of recession, it is very difficult to do this, and if the abuser is also the boss, he may write a bad reference. Sometimes, however, a bullying boss may give a good written reference to protect himself, but make negative comments if contacted by phone by a would-be employer.

Yet staying in an abusive situation will exhaust and demoralise, especially in cases of institutional, corporate or mob bullying. As with a survival plan, an exit plan should be positive rather than defeatist, e.g. looking forward to the prospect of leaving the abusive environment, or to training in something you like. Consider self-employment. Your choices will depend upon your family and financial circumstances. Make sure you understand all the financial and family resources that will sustain you as you search for a new job. Check eligibility for social welfare benefits.

Workplace bullies were once children, and the question arises of a connection between school and workplace bullying. I agree with David Yamada, Professor of Law and Director of the New Workplace Institute at the Suffolk University Law School in Boston, who suggests that children who experience abuse and trauma early in life may mistreat others when they are older. I believe that the abusive personality, created at an early life stage, is the principal common link between the two.

School bullying is as widespread as workplace bullying,

although it is difficult to define it by universal standards. Some attitudes that are seen as jokes in Spain may be viewed as insults in the UK, which heads the list of school bullying in Europe. In a survey across Europe, 27% of first level and 10% of second level students suffer bullying. The bullying highlighted in this survey was based on skin colour, language difficulties, religion and physical appearance. Britain heads the list in this survey because a large number of immigrants live there. There are widely varying statistics for the United States, but it appears that from 25% to 77% of US children experience bullying, either face to face or through cyber bullying. The most high-profile case was that of 15-year-old Phoebe Prince, who committed suicide in January 2010. This led to the criminal prosecution of a number of teenagers, and more stringent anti-bullying legislation by the Massachusetts legislature.

As with workplace abuse, school bullying can be physical, psychological, verbal and sexual, or a combination of all four. It may involve one child bullying another, a group of children against a single child, or groups against other groups. It is cruel, and involves a lack of compassion, and a lack of concern for how the victim feels. As in adult abuse, it has to do with power, control and isolation, and sometimes leads to suicide. Name calling, insults, using nicknames, being picked upon, being excluded (a frequent form of abuse among girls) are all part of school bullying. Victims are ridiculed, attacked and isolated because they are too fat, too thin, too 'stupid', too intelligent, ugly, handsome, reserved, outgoing, and so on. What is perceived as difference attracts the attention of young abusers. Students with special education needs are a significantly greater target for bullies. These include children with disabilities, such as poor sight, children who are deaf or partially deaf, and children with physical disabilities. Racism and homophobia are very much involved in bullying activities. Immigrant students, for example, can be ridiculed simply because they have a different accent or skin colour, or because of sexual orientation. Some 30% of lesbian, gay and bisexual students suffer abuse in the UK. Homosexual youths are often subject to social exclusion and psychological persecution, and they are at least four times as likely to report a serious suicide attempt. The psychologists Kimeron Hardin and Marny Hall, experts in human sexuality, remark that 'getting from childhood to adolescence, or from adolescence to adulthood can feel like running a gauntlet' for homosexual youths.

I first encountered bullying when, at the age of 12, I changed school in the late 1950s. It was a shock to be physically assaulted by two boys. Bloodied but determined, I held my own and at that young age discovered that bullies are cowardly when confronted and defeated. Today we agree that bullies are vulnerable, but that is of little consolation to a battered, demoralised victim. However, the bully and the victim both need support.

When I was a child, schools did not have anti-bullying policies, and it was 'every man for himself'. The law of the jungle prevailed, and only the hardy survived unscathed! Most schools now have such policies, and try to make being part of the school community an inclusive and positive experience. However, cyber bullying is on the increase. Children are more adept at using electronic devices than most adults, and this type of bullying can have a devastating effect on children, isolating them and making them figures of ridicule and humiliation.

When I was a school principal, my colleagues, a few parents, a few students and I drew up an anti-bullying policy, and I had to intervene in sesveral bullying episodes involving boys or girls. It always took much longer to sort out bullying by females. They tended to bring victims' families into the conflict by making insulting statements about family members, and especially about their mothers. A common insult was 'your mother is a slut and a whore'. I found, too, that girls were as likely to be involved in physical abuse as boys were.

Frequently, those children who inflict pain upon others are themselves the victims of abuse and of dysfunctional families. As with adult abusers, child bullies have particular characteristics, such as low self-esteem. They are insecure, shamed, sensitive to criticism, lack social skills, and become easily upset.

The impact of abuse on young victims is enormous. It leads to depression, and sometimes suicide. Their self-esteem is destroyed, their happiness undermined, and they become restless. I remember one victim spending an entire counselling session bent over fiddling with his shoelaces. Victims with low esteem often feel they are to blame and deserve to be abused. Bullying makes them feel worthless, hopeless and alone, and they become conscious of being different. School bullying can lead to eating disorders, cutting and anxiety. One of the worst aspects of bullying is that it can hinder students from reaching their potential, because they experience fear and no longer do their best. Their creativity is stifled. Unfortunately, some victims play the role the bullies determine for them by putting on a false front to appease them. This only increases the power of the bully over them. The abusive personality tends to torture, and will not be appeased.

One of the things I have learned as a counsellor is that the debilitating effects of bullying can be carried into adult life. The loss of self-esteem does not seem to ease with age. The psychological scars of school bullying can remain fresh and unhealed into middle age. Some children's life stories, and perhaps their identity, are defined by school bullying, and the psychological shackles remain for years, preventing them from reaching their full relationship and vocational potential. I have seen this many times with adult clients. This impact is enormously increased if the child comes from an unloving home.

It is, therefore, essential to confront bullying when it is occurring. Parents often find it difficult to do this, and fail to see the detrimental effects of bullying. Perhaps they see it as part of growing up. But, it is always necessary to be extremely sensitive to abuse, never to excuse it, and, above all, to name it. It is only when bullying becomes intolerable for their children that parents are forced to take a stand. There is also the reluctance of children to disclose that they are being bullied. They may fear the consequences of increased bullying. In Ireland, disclosure is also seen as informing, and informers have always been held up to public odium in Irish history. The tradition perhaps lingers.

It is important for parents to know how to manage a bullying report from their children. Many parents encourage the victim to react aggressively to the bullies. This is not good advice, unless, of course, as in my case, the victims are physically attacked, and must defend themselves. Otherwise, it is only encouraging physical abuse and violence. Parents should act calmly and decisively. It is important to get as much information about the bullying incident(s) as possible, and look at various ways of responding in a non-aggressive manner.

In the case of cyber bullying, help your child to keep a record of dates and times of the messages. Get them to save the messages and print them. The service provider can also block messages from certain callers. Threatening messages may warrant contacting the police. Your child may have to change his or her phone number, and on no account should abusive messages be answered. Cyber bullying may also take place through other electronic means such as computer, so parents should familiarise themselves with Facebook, tweeting, blogging and so on.

When the bully is known, the victim's parents might make a decision to meet his or her parents, and this should be done in a calm manner to avoid confrontation. It is always best to meet the school management or the teacher appointed to deal with bullying situations. Sometimes school counsellors are best placed to resolve the conflict, because they can provide a calm environment to deal with the issue. As with workplace bullying, parents may decide to remove the child from the abusive environment, but it is well to remember that bullying is universal and may arise again in the new school. In Ireland, it is part of health and safety legislation to provide for the health of the child in the school environment. This includes mental health.

Where can we find hope? I suggest the main thing that is needed is a much better sense of respect for human beings, coupled with a sense of personal responsibility. The problem is a spiritual one in a broad sense. Legislation and rules, although they may help, will not solve the problem. People must be put before profit and performance. The education system needs to be more about the person and less about results. I think that the failure of the rat race – as in the collapse of financial systems in 2009, and growing environmental problems – may lead people to ask fundamental questions and to seek to build a new type of society. I hope that this book will help to give people an awareness of the sacredness of human existence and of the person; that bullying is unacceptable in society; and from this there may be a ripple effect.

Chapter 9

Child Abuse

I looked into your eyes,
Wondering.
Famished for wombwarmth.
And all I saw was void.
A hollow wasteland.
My being screamed for love,
But barrenness raised his hand,
And kept me at distance.
I struggled in this new place.
Diminished in my hope,
And grew smaller,
And finally vanished.
Buried beneath the dungheap of rejection.
Worthless, unloved and unlovable.
And in this dark place,
Grew to hate
Myself.

Jim O'Shea

Bullying, of course, is only one aspect of child abuse. Many of the types of abuse explored above can also apply to children. Because child abuse has serious long-term effects, it deserves separate examination. A definition of child abuse normally covers four types of child mistreatment – physical abuse, sexual abuse, emotional abuse and neglect. However, I have included verbal abuse as a separate entity. This chapter, which contains shocking material, will look at these, and the immediate and long-term effects of such behaviours.

These behaviours are nauseating in any context, but particularly so in relation to precious, vulnerable and innocent children. Not only are they despicable, but they are illegal, widespread and under-reported.

It is impossible to get any reliable global statistics on child abuse, because definitions of this abuse are culturally biased. On a global level, it is estimated that 53,000 children were murdered in 2002, and an alarming number suffered physical abuse and neglect in their homes. It is reckoned that 150 million girls and 73 million boys under 18 experienced forced sexual intercourse. Almost 1 million children suffer abuse each year in the United States, 63% of these suffer from neglect, 17% from physical abuse, 9% from sexual abuse, and 7% from emotional abuse. Boys and girls are equally likely to suffer abuse, and the most targeted are the youngest age group (birth to 3 years). The majority of abused children range from 1 to 15 years old (10–15 for sexual abuse). It has been estimated that the annual cost of child abuse and neglect in the United States is over $100 billion.

In recent years we have become aware of child abuse in institutions, especially those run by some religious orders in Ireland and other countries throughout the world, by local authorities in Britain, and by institutions in the US and Canada. In the EU, and especially in eastern Europe, institutions for children are still very prevalent. One of my friends, who spent 18 years in an Irish institution, told me that the abuse suffered by inmates was akin to torture. All children are vulnerable to abuse and neglect, but children with poor health, unwanted children, those born in stigmatised conditions, and handicapped children are more at risk in institutions. Roch Longueepee, for example, reveals scandalous abuse of deaf children at a school for the deaf and blind in Canada.

Governments on a global level are taking measures with the aim of ensuring that such behaviour never occurs again. Some are more advanced in this regard, but all are culturally influenced. This can be seen in the report by Malcolm Hill and his colleagues, *International Perspectives on Child Protection.* Some countries, like Sweden, use social policies, rather than punitive measures, to promote comprehensive specialist services for families. Belgium also places emphasis on family support, but they use a multi-disciplinary approach led by a general practitioner. Currently, in Ireland, where child protection agencies are seen as chaotic and under-resourced, a new police unit is about to be established to investigate reports of sexual abuse and child neglect. The unit is a response to the Ryan report on institutional abuse, which will be mentioned later. The 2010 report by the Irish Ombudsman for Children exposed failures by the Health Service Executive to adequately protect children, especially the failure to ensure interagency co-operation, and co-operation with the police. The Ombudsman made twenty-two recommendations to eliminate these failures. The Children First guidelines drawn up by the Department of Health in 1999 have been strengthened and hopefully any failures will not recur. It is an ongoing task to combat this evil behaviour.

Developing nations have not the same level of support and children are at huge risk in these countries.

Apart from institutional abuse, we may not be aware of culturally condoned abuse. Ritualistic or satanic physical abuse (and sexual abuse) is rarely mentioned nowadays. Brian Corby in his excellent book *Child Abuse: towards a knowledge base,* briefly mentions how this abuse occurred in the US and Britain in the 1980s. There is no reason to believe that this horror has ceased.

The culture in some countries promotes particular types of ghastly physical abuse on children. Female genital mutilation is a particularly gruesome type, and can be classed as sexual abuse as well. It is a worldwide phenomenon, but the practice is mainly associated with Africa and Asia. About 130 million women have been subjected to this abomination, which involves partial or total removal of the external female genitalia, or other injury to female genital organs. Sometimes elderly women in the bush perform this procedure, without using anaesthetics or any sterile measures. It has to be reversed prior to labour, to allow delivery of a baby. It is outlawed in many countries.

In the interests of protecting our children, it is vital for us to realise that most child abuse takes place in the child's home. Child abuse in the home is grossly under-reported in developed countries, and even more so in developing countries. In the United States, it is reckoned that only one third of abuse cases are reported. Parents are hardly likely to self-report as child abusers, and children are too young, too innocent and too fearful to take action. In the United States, parents were the abusers in 77% of the confirmed cases of the 1 million child victims in 1996, and other relatives accounted for 11%.

Considering our duty as parents to protect and nurture our children, we may wonder why this happens. There is much research to answer this. We know, for example, that there is a connection between child abuse and parents with psychological or psychiatric problems; and that social stress, social isolation, low community involvement and family structure are factors in child abuse. More fundamentally, there is evidence that violence is often transmitted through generations, in which case child victims learn that abuse is normal. It is part of their malformation, and they carry a painful personal legacy, which will be looked at later in this chapter. For a minority, this legacy may be the formation of the abusive personality.

We may also wonder whether fathers or mothers are more likely to abuse their children. There is considerable confusion about this. Some studies in the United States indicate that fathers are the main abusers, while others show that 40% of child victims were abused by their mothers acting alone, 18% by fathers alone, and 17% by both parents. Brian Corby, however, asserts that the father is more likely to abuse than the mother.

One factor of great concern is that aggressive adults are the most effective models for aggression, and dependent children the most effective learners. Parents as negative models are the conductors of trans-generational abuse. Ultra-strict parents, without realising it, may be laying the foundations of abuse. The underlying tendency for abuse sown in children is reinforced by social factors, such as violence on TV, video games, and violent films or comics. There seems to be little limit now on the range of violence and physical abuse in movies.

I come from a generation where physical abuse was taken as the norm. It was not unusual for a parent, in his or her anger, to cut a stick from the ditch and beat children for disobedience. Physical abuse in school was euphemised as corporal punishment, and in my school days a beating at school would normally be reinforced by another one that evening! My father was firmly opposed to beating children, and I never suffered this extra punishment. Schools were places of terror for many pupils. I saw small children aged 5 or 6 being beaten and pinched, and having their hair pulled by frustrated teachers. I remember one girl wetting the floor with terror at the prospect of a beating. Unfortunately, we learned that physical punishment was acceptable. I was slapped at school, and when I became a teacher I slapped my pupils. There was no excuse for this, and I greatly regret ever hitting a student or any of my own children. It was control by fear, and it taught children that physical abuse was acceptable. Both teachers and parents trampled on the boundaries of young people. Young people can be exasperating and provocative in school, but beating them is not the answer.

Physical child abuse is the deliberate infliction of physical injury to a child. It involves striking children, burning, poisoning, deliberately causing them ill health, perhaps by giving them harmful substances, and shaking, pushing, pinching or biting them. Sometimes even the unborn suffer physical abuse if the mother ingests drugs such as alcohol or other substances. These can cause serious neurological and physiological damage to the unborn child. The shaken baby syndrome, whereby a frustrated caregiver shakes the baby roughly to stop it crying, is also physical abuse. The baby's neck muscles cannot support its head, and the brain bounces inside its skull leading to neurological problems and even death. Child fatalities due to physical abuse are common. A small study in America (in Lucas County, Ohio in 2007) shows that a third of fatalities from domestic violence were children. Sometimes the fatal behaviour is directed at infants. Some writers suggest that 10% of all sudden infant deaths might be due to suffocating.

There are indicators of physical abuse, although these injuries may not necessarily be from abuse. These include bruises, burning, like cigarette burns on hands or feet, rope burns from confinement, dry burns caused by an iron. There may be lacerations and skeletal injuries, such as bone fractures, stiff, swollen and enlarged joints, or head injuries with missing or loosened teeth, hair tufts missing, and jaw fracture. Internal injuries may also be a sign of child physical abuse.

Physical neglect is a facet of physical abuse. It occurs when a parent or caregiver fails to make proper provision of food, clothing, shelter, hygiene, education or medical care, although financially able or assisted to do so. It may also be reckless disregard for the child's safety, such as inattention to hazards in the home, drunk driving with children in the car and leaving a baby unattended. It also includes abandoning children without providing for their care, putting them out of the home without making such a provision, or failing to protect them from danger. Statistics show, for example, that 63% of child mistreatment in the United States is from neglect.

I believe that child neglect includes financial abuse. A child is entitled to share in a family's wealth for their support. They are financially abused when others appropriate their share for their own use. Sometimes children are forced to steal to meet the financial needs of abusers. Fagin, the 'merry old gentleman' in Dickens' novel *Oliver Twist*, is the archetypal financial abuser of children, whom he trains to be pickpockets. In real life, the author Martha Long outlines how she was forced to steal from shops, and sell butter to raise money for her mother's abusive partner.

Neglected children are often unkempt, appear unwashed, have body odour, and wear dirty, ill-fitting, ragged clothes. They may be hungry, beg for and steal food, search rubbish bins, or gulp down food when it is provided for a group. It is also suspicious if children seem abandoned, are wandering about alone, left in a car, or left alone at home. Physical ill health, chronic tiredness, infected cuts, and stunted growth may be signs of physical neglect. Babies who fail to thrive or who seem indifferent to their surroundings or to other people may be victims also.

I want readers to understand the long and short-term effects of each type of abuse on the child. Physically abused and neglected children develop a sense of worthlessness and insecurity. Ultimately, they feel unlovable. Their instinct is logical: 'if my parents do not love me, it must be my fault, and I must be unlovable'. This leads to depression, confusion about their identity, and sadness. These children find it more difficult to socialise than non-abused children. They lose trust in people, suffer from anxiety, shyness, and perform poorly in school.

The normal reaction to danger is to fight or to flee. A child cannot do this, and so they freeze their feelings, dissociate, and shut out the unbearable reality of the pain. Children split off part of themselves to hold the trauma of abuse. I believe that this psychic numbing is the most harmful effect of abuse, because it deprives children of their feelings, and makes it difficult for them to form healthy relationships in later life. They experience rage and anger at the beginning of their teens, have discipline problems in school, and eventually may drop out or be expelled. Many run away from home, become addicted to substances and alcohol, become involved in crime, and have an aggressive and hostile outlook.

We must realise, too, that children are severely affected by witnessing physical abuse directed at someone else in the home. They are indirect victims of physical abuse, and experience emotional, behavioural or physical difficulties. As an only child, I hated it when my parents fought. I hated the tension in the house, and welcomed the thaw! Children reared in an abusive environment suffer from guilt and take responsibility for the abuse. They are constantly anxious, and they may feel guilty for loving the abusive parent. They suffer fear of abandonment, can become withdrawn, blame themselves, and combine contradictory behaviours such as being needy and clinging as well as being rebellious and angry. It is likely that these children will suffer from anxiety and depression. Many children who are indirect victims of physical abuse may have problems in school. Their concentration is affected, they may have high absenteeism, have difficulties with language problems, and they do not reach their potential. They may suffer stress-related illnesses such as headaches, stomach problems, rashes, nervous ticks, nausea, vomiting, bedwetting, insomnia and eating disorders. Children who witness severe physical abuse may experience Post Traumatic Stress Disorder. Infants also suffer from severe emotional and physical problems if they are in an abusive home. They may not walk at the appropriate age, and become emotionally stunted.

Boys who witness domestic abuse are more likely to batter their partners as adults than boys raised in non-violent homes. They see it as normal.

Child abuse includes verbal abuse, and considering its potential destructiveness, I am surprised at how little is written about it. Writers in general consider it part of emotional abuse, but I believe that it deserves separate treatment. Joan Arehart-Treichel maintains that parental verbal abuse is extremely detrimental to children. We have seen how verbal abuse affects adults. I believe that the impact on children is greater, because abuse becomes part of their formation, and helps to define them. The small child has no hope of detecting verbal abuse, sees it as normal, and their self-worth is stillborn in the noxious cradle of negative comments. Our self-view is partly defined by labels, and if the labels are negative, the child will have a negative self-view or self-image. She internalises the negative messages, and the 'you are good for nothing' eventually becomes 'I am good for nothing'. Childhood verbal abuse makes us feel worthless, and many adults verbally abused as children often say to me 'I am a waste of space'.

When I explore childhood verbal abuse with adult clients, I sometimes do the 'ear exercise', whereby they draw a big ear and write in negative comments made to them as children. Comments such as 'you are useless', 'you are like your mother/father', 'you only got 90% in your test', 'you'll never be any good', are common.

I remember my mother saying 'you're a crow' when I tried to sing. She did not mean it, but it helped to define me as a singer, so when I occasionally sing nowadays I see the image of a large crow cawing. I see the funny side of this, but it illustrates how emotionally loaded words, and the images they represent, remain with us all our lives.

In her book *A Mother's Tongue,* Carolyn Denise calls verbal abuse a silent killer. She describes victims being put down and made to feel unwanted by their mothers. Verbal abuse is a deliberate behaviour that can be tailored and rationed to achieve power and control. Carolyn shows how one young victim was manipulated into losing weight through verbal abuse. When she succeeded, her mother praised her, but when her weight increased again, she was vilified and ridiculed. Another ill-advised mother praised her daughter's beauty and convinced her that her looks would garner her success in life. This mother discounted education. Her daughter's looks eventually faded, and she never reached her potential as a person, but spiralled into shame and promiscuity.

Child verbal abuse is sometimes used in more subtle ways to meet the needs of parents. The child is brainwashed, giving rise to disastrous long-term consequences. At one time, the Fourth Commandment 'honour thy father and thy mother' was a favourite way to muzzle the child, and prevent them from expressing their feelings. Guilt was often sown by the phrase 'you don't love your mother'. Eventually this guilt gives way to rage. Threats of abandonment fill a child with fear and give them a sense of not being wanted. The words 'I wish you were never born' remain imprinted in memory forever, and create a sense of being unloved.

How we communicate as parents is a fundamental formative factor in our children's development, and is passed from generation to generation. If a child learns a negative form of communication, by which it was normal to insult, berate, condemn and put down, then that child is likely to use this form of negative communication even when very young, and brings it into adulthood. This child can become a verbal bully in school and a verbal abuser in adulthood. Frequently this translates into becoming a physical bully and abuser. Verbally abused children also self-harm, behave in a delinquent way, and may become involved in anti-social behaviour, which is a serious scourge in many countries. They are likely to have problems in school, act out, and find it difficult to learn. Studies done on verbal child abuse have found that it brings on depression, anger and dissociation in adult life. These symptoms are stronger than for childhood physical abuse, and research shows that parents berating each other on an ongoing basis is more traumatic than physical abuse.

We have a duty as parents to relay positive messages to our children. Even if we suffered verbal abuse as children and see this as the normal way to communicate, we can change our verbal behaviour. The story of Imani in Naomei Will's book *Within the Walls of Silence* is a good example. Imani grew up in the 1960s, when children were 'seen and not heard'. As well as being raped as a young child and physically abused, she also suffered severe verbal abuse. She knew no other way to communicate, and had a violent adolescence. She brought her abusive ways into her marriage, and subjected her own child, Chantel, to physical and verbal abuse. Eventually, however, she made herself give affection to her child, and practised replacing hateful words with loving and healing words.

Whereas verbal abuse of children has been largely sidelined, emotional child abuse has merited more study. The latter involves behaviour that interferes with a child's mental health or social development. It systematically destroys the young human being. Emotional abusers shame children, make them feel worthless, ignore and disregard them. It is emotionally abusive to deprive children of affection and warmth, because their emotional needs are unmet. Children need to experience hugging, praise, love, support and parental mentoring. Failure to give such affection and nurture is emotional neglect, and amounts to emotional rejection of a child. The child picks up the message that they are unwanted. Of course, some mothers cannot give what they have not got, because of their own traumatic childhood. This is disastrous for the child, who feels emotionally abandoned.

If we fail to teach a child how to do ordinary things, and then blame them when they fail to do a task, we are guilty of emotional abuse. Some parents not only fail in this, but also place an adult role on their children to meet their own needs. I have encountered cases of children taking care of depressed parents, being forbidden to play with other children, and confined to the house to cater for the parent. Children are not capable of meeting parental needs, and are not equipped to perform adult roles. They will always fail, and ultimately will feel not good enough. In adulthood, this sometimes emerges as rage, shame, perfectionism and poor self-worth.

Any type of severe non-physical punishment, such as isolation from the rest of the family, is emotional abuse. Forcing children to witness or participate in inappropriate behaviour, or corrupting them (e.g. allowing them to use alcohol or drugs, or to watch cruel behaviour towards animals) comes under the umbrella of emotional abuse. It is emotionally abusive if a parent fails to intervene when the child demonstrates anti-social behaviour and refuses to seek appropriate psychological care when necessary. Indifference to a child's education, failing to enrol him, allowing him to miss too many days from school, or refusing to demand appropriate services if a child has special needs is emotional neglect. Emotionally neglected children have poor prospects for achieving their potential later in life.

Witnessing the emotional abuse of one parent by another causes severe psychological damage to the child. It undermines his harmonious development, and teaches him an unsavoury and damaging lesson. If the mother is the victim, the child may blame her, because he sees her anger, apparent weakness and vulnerability. The child may learn that women do not deserve respect, are weak, do not have power, should have no say in decision making, and should be subject to control. Alternatively, the child may feel powerless and experience great difficulty in claiming his own power in later life.

Emotional abuse has physical, behavioural, emotional and social consequences for children, because of the unhealthy and stressful atmosphere it creates in a home. It may slow physical development, lead to eating disorders, create speech problems, and lead to self-harm and suicidal behaviour. It may also prevent infants from thriving. It can affect a child's intelligence, memory, attention and moral development. It breeds low self-worth, irritability, sadness, withdrawal and depression. This depression can bring up suicidal thoughts. Child victims may also suffer from alienation, personality disorders, neediness, flashbacks and nightmares.

Most seriously, emotional abuse can freeze the emotions, leading to a pain-filled, restless and lonely life as adults, when being in a warm intimate relationship proves uncomfortable or impossible. They are 'burned' by intimacy, and withdraw in confusion. Emotionally abused children lose their sense of trust in others, when they cannot trust those who are supposed to be caring for them. When a mother is emotionally distant and the father is abusive, the consequences are lethal. The child builds a shell and freezes his feelings. When feelings are frozen the self is punished, and this has been aptly described as soul murder or psychic murder. Emotional abuse brings with it feelings of inadequacy and worthlessness.

Effects that are even more devastating arise from sexual abuse, a serious crime and I believe the most damaging of all abusive behaviours. Sexual abuse of children is particularly appalling. It is a silent, hidden crime that robs children of innocence, and is global and common. It exists among all social classes, although most reported incidents come from poorer families. The statistics are disquieting. It is estimated that one third of sexually abused children never disclose the experience to anyone. We know, however, that up to 30% of girls and 23% of boys suffer some form of sexual abuse. Canadian reports estimate that 6 out of 10 victims of sexual assault are under 17.

Sexually abusive behaviour is wide ranging. It can be covert or masked by the pretence that it is caring for the child, for example fondling when washing the child, or teaching the facts of life in such a manner as to receive sexual gratification for it. The child does not see this as sexual abuse, but it has a profoundly negative effect, and often it is only in therapy that it is labelled for what it is – sexual abuse. The real test of sexual abuse is that it has a sexual purpose.

Mic Hunter's book *Abused Boys* gives a comprehensive account of the various types of sexual abuse. It also contains stories from people who were sexually abused as children. Some of these include indecent exposure, touching the child in a sexual manner, and using sexualised conversation. Some abusers get sexual pleasure by making the child dress in over-revealing clothes, stripping and spanking him/her, by inappropriate kissing, or making the child watch another being sexually abused, or by sexualising the relationship between the child and a pet. Some abusers make children watch pornographic material, or partake in pornographic videos, expose them to an act of sexual intercourse between others, masturbate in their presence, force them to have oral sex, and penetrate them with objects or with a finger. Using the internet to groom children for sexual activity is also sexual abuse.

Putting children into prostitution is a particularly heinous form of abuse. The great majority of these children suffer sexual abuse at home, before being put on the street. Studies show that child prostitution is a serious problem in some countries. For example, in Canada it is estimated that up to 80% of those involved in the sex industry began as sexually abused children.

Rape is the most serious form of child sexual abuse, and there are revolting incidences of small babies being raped. Jim Hopper, an American psychologist knowledgeable on sexual abuse, estimated in one of his studies that 1 in 6 boys are sexually abused before the age of 16. One of the most disturbing stories on child rape is that of Sophia McColgan, told by Susan McKay. Sophia and her siblings, who lived in the west of Ireland, were raped by their father over a twenty-year period. Her sickening ordeal began when she was only 6, and is narrated in the book *Sophia's Story*.

The revelations of the Murphy and Ryan reports on the sexual abuse of children in Irish institutions or by paedophilic Irish clergy are shocking. Global reports on institutional and clerical abuse are equally shocking, especially in the US, Canada, Australia, New Zealand, Britain and Europe. Institutional abuse in Ireland was mainly by religious, and was on a grand scale attracting much publicity. It thrived on unlimited power over poverty-stricken children, and was unhindered because of neglect by various agencies, such as the Department of Education, the Department of Justice, the police, and health services. Reports to government were not published in the media, and an ex-Taoiseach (Prime Minister) finally apologised for the state's failure to prevent this awful abuse. The relationship between the Catholic Church and the Irish state, whereby clergy and religious had extensive power and were held in deference, facilitated this abuse.

On a global level, clerical sexual abuse was not reined in, and paedophile priests were shifted from parish to parish, allowing them to continue their abuse. Ireland has been in the spotlight for the last few years, and the torturous efforts to bring closure to this unspeakable saga have brought immense pain to victims there. The wounds of victims are extremely raw, and will remain so, until they feel that sufficient reparation, full acknowledgement, full accountability and an acceptable apology have been made. Their wounds are also kept raw by the drip feed of sexual abuse revelations that occur on a frequent basis. I hope that closure can be brought to this suffering, and we will never again have to read the gruesome details of how children were abused by those in authority, who had a powerful sense of entitlement and power. It is to be welcomed that many of these children, long forgotten, have emerged as adults to reclaim some power. Many, unfortunately, have become alcoholics or committed suicide. I have no doubt, too, that religious and clergy who had no part in this dreadful story and who had no knowledge that it was happening will find some relief from their own discomfort, if it is finally 'resolved'. I have spoken to victims, however, who feel that these clergy should have spoken in support of sufferers when knowledge of clerical abuse became widespread.

In recent years, we have become aware of children being abused by sports coaches, although much more research is required. When we consider the large number of young people involved in sport, the statistics for those who experienced some type of sexual abuse are shocking. A 2004 study of female athletes in Norway shows that 51% experienced sexual harassment. A 1993 study in the UK found that 43% of female athletes were subject to sexual abuse, and a study in Australia found that 31% of female and 21% of male athletes were sexually abused. Similar statistics are available for other countries.

Only recently have governments focused on child protection in sport. The UK was the first country to establish a specific centre for this. The denial of clerical abuse was mirrored by similar denial of abuse by sports coaches. Any mention of sexual abuse in a sport's context was taboo, because of a set of beliefs about sport. There was a fundamental belief that sport was a morally pure type of behaviour embodying the principle of fair play. One dangerous belief was that of male privilege over females. Parents need to be aware that talented athletes are more at risk of sexual grooming and abuse than others. Celia Brackenridge, an expert on aspects of sexual abuse in sport, argues that the power balance changes in favour of coaches as talented athletes reach the 'training to win' stage. Abuse in sport runs on a continuum, partly facilitated by the intimacy of the coach or mentor with athletes. This intimacy moves from non-abusive behaviour to grooming and the gradual lowering of the athletes' boundaries, and finally to sexual abuse. Much depends on the vulnerability of the athlete, the inclinations of the coach, and the opportunities within the sporting organisation to abuse.

What is shocking about abuse by sports coaches, and particularly clerical sexual abuse, is that so few have abused so many. However, despite our pain and rage when reading these reports, it is important in the interests of child protection to realise that at least 80% of child sexual abuse is perpetrated by family members – parents (including foster parents), grandparents, uncles, aunts, cousins, siblings, as well as close family friends, strangers, and people in authority. It is worrying that a large number of sexual abusers attempt or commit their first sexual assault by the age of 16.

Sexual abuse within the family (incest) is a hidden sickness, facilitated by isolation and threats. Mic Hunter classifies incestuous fathers in several ways. The most common type of abuser is the one who is dependent on his family to satisfy his sexual and emotional needs. This type is over-controlling and preoccupied with sex. The next most common is psychopathic, has little emotional connection to his victims and is promiscuous. The others are psychotic, drunken, paedophilic, mentally defective and highly stressful men. Alcohol, as already mentioned, does not create the sexual abuse, but makes it more likely to happen, as inhibitions are lowered. A paedophile (Greek word meaning 'one who loves children') is attracted to prepubescent children as sex partners. Psychiatrists see it as a psychological disorder of being obsessed with children. In recent years, it is considered by some as an addiction, and now many researchers see it as an aspect of neural development. Paedophiles are a minority of sexual abusers.

Family members use different tactics to gain sexual power and control over the child. Some use threats of harming the victim, or stoke the child's fear of abandonment by telling her that she will be left alone if the perpetrator is jailed. On the other hand, a child may be bribed, or told that he is special. A child needs love, and abuse may be masked by this ruse. One particularly insidious form of abuse is non-sexual incest, whereby a parent treats a child as a surrogate spouse, subconsciously feeding his or her needs off the child. This tactic involves the mother pleading that no woman is good enough for her son, and ridiculing prospective partners. This is a possible sign of enmeshment.

Sexual abuse by a family member means the home is no longer a sanctuary. This is particularly torturous where the abuser is a parent, because the parent will have made every effort to create a semblance of trust, and when it is shattered the effect is more severe. It is an equally bleak picture if the home has never been a place of safety, but of neglect and coldness.

Research indicates that child sexual abuse is mainly perpetrated by men. Neither can we assume that sexual abuse in lone parent families is committed by mothers. Children may be more at risk from visiting males in such family structures. Nevertheless, apart from rape, we now believe that female sexual abuse of children is higher than reported, although research into this is in its infancy. The rate of reporting of female perpetrators is low. Research by the Office of Justice Programs in the US holds that females are responsible for 3% of rape, 5% of other violent sex offences, and 19% of non-violent sex offences. At any one time about 140,000 men and 1,500 women are in prison for sexual offences in the US.

The minority abused by mothers experience a greater loss of trust and enormous betrayal. They experience shame, guilt and self-loathing. Sometime it takes victims of female perpetrators years to realise that they have been sexually abused. This is partly because of traditional nonchalant attitudes towards male victims of female abusers, and partly because much of the abuse is cunning, and masks the abuse.

But the impact of sexual abuse on children, irrespective of the gender of the perpetrator, is enormous. Jim Hopper, however, cautions that children suffer ill effects from many non-sexual sources, and when evaluating the effects of sexual abuse on them, advises that all experiences should be considered. In relation to sexual abuse, he makes the point that the age of the child is important, and the younger the child the more damaging the effects of the abuse are. He also argues that the abuse has greater effects when parents, or people trusted by the child, are the abusers. When the child's disclosure is not believed, the negative impact of the abuse is increased. If the child has been subjected to humiliation and ridicule, this, too, increases the impact. Some sexual abusers use other depraved behaviours after a rape to humiliate the child. This is a sign of entitlement and power.

The child seeks love and gets abuse. It needs love and gets cruelty. The child's psyche withers in the barrenness of rejection, as it carries the fear created by its powerlessness and inability to defend its boundaries. Sexual abuse can bring on eating disorders, depression, suicidal thoughts, as well as addiction, anxiety, withdrawal, nightmares and somatic complaints. Many of the symptoms of Post Traumatic Stress Disorder, such as hypervigilance, sometimes manifest themselves due to sexual abuse. Sexually abused children may experience a wide range of feelings such as fear, anxiety and depression. They will be angry, hostile and aggressive. They may be involved in self-destructive behaviour, feel isolated, have poor self-esteem, and find it difficult to trust others.

Because of the confusion and fear raised in the abused child, any touch or physical tenderness may be interpreted as sexual, and bring on fear. Severe sexual abuse may also cause the child to dissociate and freeze. When victims dissociate from their feelings, they compartmentalise the abuse, go into a trance, and shut out the violation of their bodies. This reaction can be seen in Martha Long's witty but sad account of her physical and sexual abuse in her book *Ma, He Sold Me for a Few Cigarettes*. This defence mechanism may become a permanent way of dealing with trauma, and may be carried into adulthood, with fatal consequences for intimate relationships.

Dissociation is also reflected in self-harm, commonly known as cutting, but includes burning, scratching and biting oneself. Generally, people who cut are in a trance-like state as they turn inwards from connecting to others. Steven Levenkron, in his book *Cutting: understanding and overcoming self-mutilation*, asserts that the first incident of cutting begins with strong feelings of anger, anxiety or panic. Globally, the numbers involved in self-harm are staggering. In the US, at least 2 million people are self-injurers. In the European Union, it has been found that 3 in 10 girls and 1 in 10 boys self-harm. Boys use lethal methods. Cutting generally begins in adolescence, and often extends into adulthood. It is short-term relief from the constant feeling of emotional pain resulting from sexual abuse, and is an external manifestation of this suffering. It may also be an act of anger towards the abuser.

One of Steven Levenkron's narrators told him that it was like medicine for her fears, because the psychological pain of the abuse is greater than the pain of the mutilation. Cutting also gives the victim control over who inflicts the pain, in contrast to the powerlessness experienced when being raped. The physical pain of the mutilation also releases endorphins, which are opiate-like substances produced by the brain to kill pain. It is easy to see how people could become addicted to the release of this substance by self-inflicted pain. Self-mutilators also get relief from seeing the blood seeping from their wound.

It can be argued that cutting is a cry for help, but it is also likely that the sense of shame engendered by abuse may be magnified by the shame of cutting, and hinders disclosure about the abuse. These feelings are increased as the victim further withdraws from human contact and is imprisoned in fear of rejection. They find it difficult to confide in their families. It robs children of self-esteem and self-worth, and damages their trust in people, making them see the world as a hostile place. This is increased if the child is infected following sexual assault, because occasionally this can result in the getting a sexually transmitted disease such as herpes, gonorrhoea or syphilis.

Sexual abuse fills a child with shame, and they bring this into adulthood. Shame is a powerful and painful sense of the self being damaged and worthless. The feeling of shame can be intensified if the child experiences physical arousal and pleasure from the abuse. This applies to both boys and girls. Feelings of arousal and pleasure create guilt, confusion and self-loathing.

All humans have to negotiate the difficult challenges of life stages, from birth until death. The abused child, however, not only has to survive the challenges of childhood and adolescence, but also must carry the burden of the abuse. It is a heavy burden, and distracts the child from dealing with normal developmental tasks, such as becoming independent, creating a unique identity, having a sense of achievement, and nurturing self-esteem. If you want a comprehensive exploration of sexual child abuse at the various life stages from infancy onwards, I suggest you read Felicia Ferrara's book *Childhood Sexual Abuse: developmental effects across the lifespan*.

As we have seen when looking at boundaries, adolescence is a time of intense sexual change, and these normal changes become entangled with the impact of sexual abuse. Instead of being seen as normal, they are now infused with the shame that sexual abuse engenders in the adolescent. Emotional reactions at bodily changes are severely charged by such abuse. Sexual abuse of adolescents also brings the risk of pregnancy, an added element of trauma for the developing female. A high number of pregnant teenagers have abortions, and this too can bring its own trauma.

It is also highly likely, and increasingly a worry, that sexual abuse can make a child sexually active at an early age, and become promiscuous. Promiscuity leads to a high risk of getting a sexually transmitted disease. Paradoxically, adults abused as children may come to see their value only as a sexual object. Therefore, while fearing sex, they may also feel rejected if they are rebuffed in an intimate relationship.

Sexually abused children bring emotional turmoil to adulthood, and may be consumed by intense shame, guilt and rage. It is little wonder that many suffer from depression, feel suicidal, and become addicted to alcohol and abuse substances. Many survivors of sexual abuse develop personality disorders and suffer from anxiety, low self-esteem and a sense of worthlessness. They have been used and abused as children and feel unlovable, often have a poor body image, and feel anxious in intimate relationships.

Sexual abuse of boys has particular consequences. Masculinity is stereotyped as dominating, fearless and tough. The shame, rage and sense of worthlessness that a raped boy brings to adulthood are difficult to imagine. He struggles with a plethora of debilitating feelings such as fear, inadequacy and alienation. He may be beset by sexuality issues, such as sexual dysfunction and confusion over sexual orientation. I have never met a person sexually abused in childhood who did not have a negative outlook about others and about himself. They generally feel helpless and isolated, and many use alcohol to dull the pain. There is also a strong risk of suicide. Adult male survivors of childhood sexual abuse experience self-blame, guilt, shame, humiliation. They may become anxious, depressed and find it difficult to relate. It is likely that they will have low self-esteem, and possibly symptoms of Post Traumatic Stress Disorder.

Sometimes their behaviour as adults is to emphasise their masculinity in order to negate the turmoil boiling within. Risky behaviour such as sexual promiscuity, crime or aggressive acts may become habitual. They construct a facade of bravery, strength and success, while the inner emasculated child cringes in terror. How exhausting it is to keep up this facade, and to keep the helpless child hidden. Ironically, this is sometimes done by deflection away from themselves and becoming involved in helping others.

Mike Lew, in his book *Victims No Longer,* raises the issue of loss. It is a good way to look at the impact of child sexual abuse. The victim loses his childhood, loses memory of his childhood (as a defence mechanism), loses the ability to relate and properly socialise, loses the chance to play, to learn, to be happy and peaceful, to defend his or her boundaries, to be nurtured, and much, much more. In the case of clerical and institutional abuse, the victims also suffer a spiritual loss, a loss of faith, and of trust in their church.

Considering this painful legacy, it is important that parents, teachers, social workers and people in authority should be aware of signs of child sexual abuse. These may vary with the age of the child, although they do not always indicate sexual abuse *per se*. For younger children, there may be inappropriate sexual activity such as excessive curiosity about sex, promiscuous behaviour, and sexual acting out with other children. Sexually abused children may find it difficult to sleep, and frequently wet the bed. Inevitably, many have learning problems, cling to their mothers, and develop psychosomatic disorders. Pre-puberty and early teenage children may become passive and withdrawn, and bathe excessively. They may have sexual references in school-work, and be aggressive or depressed. There are serious warning signs such as refusing to change clothes in front of others, stained or bloody underclothing, bruises or bleeding on the external genitalia or anal areas, and preoccupation with sexual organs. With older children, there may be suicide attempts, early marriage, running away, pregnancy, substance abuse, and carrying out illegal acts.

In this age of technology, parents should also be highly alert to sexual abuse via the internet. Children spend a considerable amount of time at the computer, and those who use the internet are targets for sexual abusers and risk becoming sexualised at an early age. Government-supported research in Ireland shows that 33% of 9–16-year-old children have been approached on the internet by people who asked them for personal information such as photographs, phone numbers, addresses and the names of the schools they attend. Three out of every 10 said that their parents never check up on them while they are online, and half revealed that their parents did not use filtering software to block unsavoury sites. Many also said that their parents knew less about the internet than they did. Hence, it is important that parents become computer literate, so that they can negotiate the computer activities of their children. It is always worth checking the computer, and the internet history, to see if there is any pornography on it. Looking at phone bills is also recommended, as they may indicate that the child is making phone calls, especially long distance ones. They should investigate unfamiliar phone numbers. Another warning sign is if a child receives mail and packages from people that the parents do not know. It is also worth investigating if the child turns off the monitor or changes the screen quickly if a parent enters the room. The child becoming withdrawn from the family may also be a sign of internet sexual abuse. Finally, it is worth checking if a child is using an online account belonging to someone else.

There is no excusing sexual abuse. Sexual abusers are seen as having a sickness. That may be so, but sexually abusive behaviour is a choice, and there is a moral and serious responsibility to make the opposite choice of respecting the child rather than using them to fulfil sexual needs, and inflicting on them lifelong pain.

I began this chapter on how precious our children are. Our duty of care and our responsibility involves not only protecting them from an abusive environment, but the creation of a positive, nurturing one that affirms them, and sows the seeds of self-confidence and a strong identity in them. In order to do this we must begin with respect, the very opposite of abuse. If we give our children respect, love, attention, empathy, honesty, and allow them appropriate independence, they will embody these traits as adults. We only need be 'good enough' parents, and I cannot find a better explanation of what a 'good enough' parent is, than the thoughts enshrined in the beautiful poem by Mary Rita Korzan, *When You Thought I Wasn't Looking:*

When you thought I wasn't looking,
You hung my first painting on the refrigerator
And I wanted to paint another one.

When you thought I wasn't looking,
You fed a stray cat,
And I thought it was good to be kind to animals.

When you thought I wasn't looking,
You baked a birthday cake just for me,
And I knew that little things were special things.

When you thought I wasn't looking,
You said a prayer,
And I believed there is a God I could always talk to.

When you thought I wasn't looking
You kissed me good-night
And I felt loved.

When you thought I wasn't looking,
I saw tears come from your eyes,
And I learned that sometimes things hurt –
But it's all right to cry.

When you thought I wasn't looking,
You smiled
And it made me want to look that pretty too.

When you thought I wasn't looking
You cared
And I wanted to be everything I could be.

When you thought I wasn't looking
I looked . . .
And I wanted to say 'thanks'
For all those things you did
When you thought I wasn't looking.

Chapter 10

Remaining in or Leaving
an Abusive Relationship

Shackled forever?
Never to leave the prison?
Never to find the key?
Never to breathe the air of freedom?
Never to find self-expression?
Never to be?
Always lost?
Always leashed?
Always rejected?
Never loved?
Always caring for the unlovable?
No escape from lash of tongue?
From invisible restraint?
From unwilling surrender?
Never to seek another place?

Jim O'Shea

Leaving or staying in an abusive relationship is a decision. Linda articulates it well when she says that she can choose to

> ... live a horrible life, and expose my son to it too, because I was too afraid to leave, or get out and struggle in the world as a single parent, where I could start building a new life, and every day get a little bit further in our new life, and give a loving childhood to my son, so he can grow to be a good man.

Many women leave and return a number of times during the calm part of the abusive cycle. Eventually they learn through painful experience that the abuser does not change, as the cycle of violence begins again. Linda went from being optimistic during the calm period, to distress at the abandonment she and Jack endured within a short time of returning.

> We were about a month and a half back together, and I was happy, because he was really making an effort. But, slowly things went back to the old ways. He went off every evening, and although he didn't stay out all night, he returned very late. I remember one evening he went off with one of his friends, who called to the house. He said that he would be back around 11, but I went to bed at 10 or so. At 2am, I heard him come home, and got up and asked where he had been until this hour. He said that he was just chatting to his friend, and that he didn't realise that the time had gone so quickly. I was so tired from hurting, and I was back with him to make a go of it again; I didn't want to believe that he was being unfaithful again, so I swallowed his story and went to bed. I guess you could say I was living in denial.
>
> I remember telling him that we were spending no time together, and that Jack hardly ever saw him. He didn't listen. One evening when he was going out again, I was crying and pleaded with him to stay. I knew deep inside what was going on. I just didn't want to believe it. He left that evening, and my last memory of him was walking out the door, and I felt so on my own. Because I *was* on my own. I was on my own in this relationship, and I was on my own with regard to the love in our relationship, because I was the only one that loved.

I recognise that it takes strength to stay or leave. Women's Rural Advocacy Programs (WRAP), an American organisation, outlines a long list of why women stay in abusive relations. WRAP sees three type of reasons – situational factors, emotional factors, and personal beliefs, a powerful combination that makes it so difficult to leave an abusive relationship.

As a victim, you may harbour a whole range of fears based on your situation. You possibly fear the legal road you may have to take to disentangle the strands of your marriage. The system is adversarial and centred around the legal profession itself rather than the clients. I have seen wealthy clients who paid enormous sums to lawyers, who are reluctant to advise them on other approaches such as collaborative family law. This latter process provides a couple with the opportunity to resolve their separation issues without the threat of going to court. Lawyers and their clients meet on a number of occasions and work out a settlement that meets, as far as possible, their priorities, goals, needs and interests. It is less expensive than using the court. You might also consider mediation, which is free. Details of how this works are on the internet. However, since it involves parity and equality in coming to an agreement, I would be surprised if your abusive partner went with this option.

I have no doubt that you clearly understand the damage an abusive environment does to your children, but you may remain because you worry that the emotional damage to them may be greater if you separate. You may also be fearful of losing custody. You may be aware of survivors who went through the courts, and who were not in any way emotionally supported.

Apart from dreading the legal process, you may also fear the unknown, such as constructing a new life, and making formidable life changes. Linda briefly outlines her fears.

> So yes, I would say to anyone it is the hardest thing to do
> – because you still love the man you leave! You are so
> afraid of the unknown. You don't know how you will
> manage financially; don't know where you will live.
> Everything is unknown. But it had to be done, and I am
> glad God gave me the courage and guidance to do it, or
> I'd still be stuck in the rut of a loveless home and
> marriage!

Perhaps you also fear the physical danger to yourself or your children if you try to leave. You may feel like prey, and are terrified of being hunted down, or of the abuser calling to your workplace. This apprehension is well justified. Frequently, when an abuser learns of the victim's decision to leave his fury erupts, and there are cases when the threat to their lives is so great that they have to flee, and leave their children behind. Research shows that a battered woman is at a 75% greater risk of being murdered after leaving the relationship than those who stay. The reason for this is not about the anger aroused in the abuser, but in his loss of control and power over the survivor. It is almost like a drug addict being deprived of his 'fix'.

Each situation is different, but perhaps like many women you are financially dependent on your partner. It might be that you cannot afford to rent a house, and it is true that in many countries there may not be sufficient hostels or refuges for fleeing women and their children. The booklet *Lean on Me: an information guide for women living with domestic abuse* lists women's refuges and support services in Ireland. These services are run by voluntary boards and are part-funded by the health service.

Sadly, you may not have the support of your family, who may see separation or divorce as a scandal, and they may try to pressurise you to remain in the abusive relationship for the sake of 'respectability'. It is also very difficult to leave friends and neighbours. There is every chance that you feel isolated and powerless, especially if the abuser's family is powerful and well connected.

There are also many powerful emotional factors influencing the decision to stay. Sometimes, it is because the full impact of abuse renders women incapable of leaving. They become exhausted, and are almost mentally paralysed from sheer terror, and from being in a state of continuous anxiety. Because of the controlling and sometimes physical nature of abuse, victims may also feel trapped. Others become emotionally dependent because they lack self-esteem, and, at another level, victims bond with perpetrators through the trauma, and this, too, leads to emotional dependence.

Even if you are not bonded with your abuser through trauma, you may harbour a whole plethora of emotions that ties you to the relationship. At the time of marriage, for example, you pledged loyalty to the abuser, and this lingers even in the presence of abuse. You may, like Linda, blind yourself to the reality and make excuses for your tormentor. It is not easy to abandon the emotional investment in the relationship, and, like some victims, you may see the hidden, hurt child in the abuser, and a rescuing urge is magnified as you become aware of his vulnerability, depression and loneliness. It seems as if you are abandoning a vulnerable child.

I have no doubt that you have experienced loneliness and rejection in your abusive relationship, and it is understandable that you may not wish to add to your sense of loneliness, and stall at the prospect of being abandoned and alone, of losing a relationship or the friendship of the abuser's family, whom you may have liked. Staying may also indicate a denial or a reluctance on your part to admit that the relationship has failed, and a hope that it might be salvaged. It may be that an abusive environment was normal because of your childhood experience, and you have been unintentionally conditioned by a parent-victim to remain in the relationship.

Religious beliefs and personal values are very powerful influences in shaping the decision to stay. St Paul did women no favours in his concept of female subservience to men, who may have been conditioned by the Pauline teaching to see themselves as being the authority figures. On the other hand, many victims find that prayer helps them to leave when they realise that they have no feelings for the abuser.

One of the most powerful personal values is the belief that children need both parents. Many victims have a strong sense of duty and responsibility, and a belief that marriage is forever. When you add this to traditional female socialisation, you have a powerful guilt recipe for holding a woman in the relationship. Women were taught to believe that they have the responsibility of keeping the family together, or that suffering is the path to salvation. Living with the abusive man is the cross she must carry, and she does her utmost to fulfil her 'role' of making her partner happy, while keeping up the pretence of a successful marriage with two parents to care for their children. Look at Linda's mindset as her marriage deteriorated:

> I was so upset. What was I going to do? I couldn't have a failed marriage. I couldn't tell my parents and friends and the general community that I had a failed marriage. I couldn't let my son come from a broken home. That was not my plan for him. He had to come from a home with two parents. And how could I ever leave Stephen? God knows what he would do if he didn't have me to lean on! So who was I kidding thinking I was leaving? I had chosen to get married, so I had to get on with it, and hope it would get better. So I plodded along and every day carried the weight of the world on my shoulders, and played happy families to the outside world, including my family. I would put on a false smile and make out everything was great. But you can only carry so much for so long! I was slowly getting worn out!

So she resolved to be a 'better wife', a behaviour that many abused women use. She may not have understood the abusive mindset at the time, but she soon came to realise that it was a fruitless effort.

> Who was I kidding – you need two people in a marriage. One person putting in the effort is not going to make a blind bit of difference. He wasn't reading from the same hymn sheet as me.

I am convinced that one of the most potent influences on remaining in an abusive relationship is the confusion that arises because of the Jekyll and Hyde personality of the abuser. The ten types of abusive personalities mentioned by Lundy Bancroft contain plausible and kind traits. Partners may see only those qualities, and are blind to the controlling, wounding elements. This can be reinforced by the reaction of the abusers, who may plead, promise to change, enter therapy, apologise, or threaten to commit suicide. Others, however, increase their abusive control, and make their partners powerless by making them pregnant as often as possible, removing birth control devices and forcing themselves upon them.

Finally, psychologists suggest that a primary reason for remaining in abusive relationships is the failure of victims to mourn and accept their losses. You might surmise that escaping from severe abuse is a liberating loss, but there can be confusion because feelings about a partner are so mixed.

Many of the above factors apply to male victims also. I have seen cases of severe emotional and physical abuse of males, who tell me that they endure it because they love the perpetrator. Men are as conscious of the wellbeing of their children as women are, and many remain because they incorrectly believe that they can deflect the violence from their children. I know of several cases where wives bluntly told their husbands 'I will allow you to remain on my terms only'. This in effect meant strict control, where all contact with the partner's family is totally severed. Many men also stay because they have become used to a comfortable standard of living, and fear the prospect of poverty.

This is a well-justified fear. In many countries, men are vulnerable in legal separation cases, and I have known several male victims who were pauperised by separation, and could barely afford to rent an apartment. Of course, if a wife devotes her time to looking after her children, it is only fair and right that her ex-husband must support her. However, I also know men whose ex-wives are professionally qualified, earned a living before marriage, did not have children, and were granted substantial maintenance by the courts. The sums involved were ruinous to the ex-husbands.

Male socialisation can be as relevant a factor as female socialisation in the context of having an abusive relationship. Many men are conscious of how society might view them if it was seen that they were fleeing from physical abuse. They also rightly fear losing their children in a custody battle, where women are generally favoured by the courts. Some of my clients were denied reasonable access to their children because perpetrators told lies about them in court. There is a support group in Ireland for male victims, appropriately named AMEN, which is a voluntary organisation. It provides a confidential helpline and a support service and information.

Just as belonging to particular minority groups sometimes attracts abusiveness, it can also create difficulties in leaving. Physically handicapped people may have become dependent on the abuser. Ethnic minorities face obstacles and problems if they decide to leave. They may not find the same social support as others, and for some minority groups it is seen as unforgiveable to leave a spouse. Services specifically for fleeing gay people are severely limited. Lesbians may not find a safe place because shelters are equally open to their abusers. There are even fewer safe places for gay men.

While recognising why people remain in abusive relationships, I consider it unethical as a counsellor to support them over a long period in such a relationship. The role of the counsellor is for the well-being of his clients, and I think it is wrong to collude with them in remaining in a toxic environment. However, leaving is a long, painful and difficult process. Elaine Weiss's stories reveal that some women remain for years in abusive relationships. One survivor put it at 8 years, 7 months and 21 days. I believe that my role as a counsellor is to listen to my client's story, empathise with their suffering, educate them on abuse, challenge them about remaining a victim, and assist them if they decide to leave. Fortunately, as Sandra Horley reminds us, 88% of abused women leave following repeated assaults. It would probably be true to say that victims leave when staying becomes unendurable and it becomes less painful to leave than to stay. Linda puts it well when she says:

> The decision to leave was the hardest, most devastating, decision of my life. Jack and I lost our home, and our possessions. I lost my husband who despite everything, I

still loved and cared for. And like I predicted he got worse when I left. He didn't work at all, but went on welfare, and lost all respect for himself and everything around him.

Yet, however devastating it is, there are good reasons for leaving. It is appropriate to leave if the perpetrator refuses to admit that he/she is being abusive, continues to abuse, and is unwilling to get help. You owe it to yourself to look for some type of peace and happiness outside the abusive home. If you are being devalued, and treated as worthless, life is hardly worth living.

Linda decided to leave when her husband said that he would assault her father, who had confronted him about his behaviour. This threat seemed to make her realise that Stephen did not love her.

I am extremely close to my father, and my husband knows that. Yet he was willing to hurt my beloved father, and didn't care about me, and how that would make me feel, or didn't care about my dad – a man nearly three times his age. I was sick to my stomach when I heard that. How could my husband, who was supposed to love me so much, threaten to physically hurt one of the most important people in my life? I think those few words he said that night on the phone about my father really set things clear in my head. He didn't care about me. He was just an angry man, ready to inflict that anger on a man who was so good to him in the past. My father often got work for him, when he had none, and helped him out as much as he could. I left him the next day for the first time.

If there are children involved, I believe that it is imperative to leave. Some people, including some researchers, feel that it is better to leave children in an abusive parental relationship than suffer the trauma of leaving and losing a parent. I do not agree with this view. I strongly believe that if children are in the presence of any type of continuing abuse, they should be removed, before serious psychological or emotional damage is done. As I showed earlier, the longer they are left the greater the harm they will suffer. Children are like sponges. They absorb the tension, anger, hostility and fear in an abusive home. I am greatly concerned when I see children who have become withdrawn, fearful, anxious and insecure as they constantly witness the acrimony between their parents. Not only are these children deprived of happiness and contentment, but they also have poor role models in abusive parents. Non-abusive parents, like Linda, are very conscious of the potential damage to their children.

> As much as I thought about Jack coming from a broken home, he was already in a broken home. I couldn't have my son grow up and see his father call me a 'bitch' or a 'cunt', which were commonly said to me. I was so fearful for my son and his future that I didn't want him emotionally damaged from what he saw or heard. There was little love in the house in the end, and it was unfair to bring him up in a house full of tension, and so unstable.

Her fears for Jack's emotional safety increased when Stephen physically abused her. On one occasion when he raged and destroyed furniture, she made the decision to permanently remove her child from the abusive environment.

> He pushed me out of the way to get inside. He grabbed my arms so tight and pushed. I had marks left on my arms that day from him. I followed him and told him to get out. He kicked things around the kitchen, kicked the clothes-horse to the other side of the room. He was shouting and was in a complete rage. His face turned red. He then went to the bedroom and started pulling the wardrobe doors off in anger, and throwing them across the room. My son was sitting in his high chair when all this was going on, screaming with fright. I told Stephen to get out, that I was calling the gardaí and that I was leaving. But he didn't calm down. When he had his damage done, he went out the front door and sped off in his van with the tyres screeching. I ran and locked the front and back doors, and I called the gardaí. About 5 minutes later, he came back.

The doors were locked, and he told me to open the doors or he would break the glass, as the back door was a patio sliding glass door. I told him that I had called the gardaí, and he said to me 'of course you did, you twisted bitch'. This was crazy – how can he be calling me twisted, when he has done all this? He blamed me for this, just as he did for everything.

Even if abusers are only targeting a partner, there is always the possibility that in time they will begin to abuse their children. It is worthwhile recalling that emotional and verbal abuse often lead to physical violence. Firstly, it may be a push or a shove, then a blow or a kick, and finally severe beatings. Abuse invites retaliation, which, however justified, intensifies the tension and hatred in the home, and children cannot survive emotionally in such an atmosphere.

Many victims leave when they begin to see the pattern that underpins abuse, and the deliberate campaign to undermine and control becomes apparent. One of my clients compared it to a jigsaw. When the jigsaw is fragmented victims are lost in confusion, but as the pieces are assembled, they become clear that it is not healthy or wise to stay. Very often sufferers decide to leave during the third stage of the abusive cycle, when the release of violent anger by the abuser brings about calm, and the appearance of love and warmth. But when the abuser learns of this decision, the fury aroused makes it necessary to create a safety plan. This will vary from person to person and country to country, although there are some basic ingredients of a 'survival kit'.

One of these is having sufficient finance to support you and your children, if any. I advise opening a separate bank account or hiding money until the time of leaving. The difficulties in this will be determined by the level of control the abuser has on the home's finances. Linda successfully took this precaution.

When things were bad, sometimes at night I started making plans. At the time, they felt like things to keep in my head just in case. I never thought I'd use them, because things would be getting better! I set up a credit union account that he didn't know about, and for months I put little bits of money into it. Initially it was set up to save because he could go off some weekends, and wouldn't give me any of his wages to do the shopping, and I would be short. It was a safe haven financially for me. But really it was the starting point of my planning to live without him. Up to then I had never kept anything from him, but I kept that account from him, as it was a means to survival for my son and me, and I had to think of us, when he would go away and leave us.

It is vital for you to prearrange a safe place to recuperate, and eventually plan a new life. Creating a new life means having relevant documentation, and so it is essential to copy important documents, and give them to a friend for safekeeping.

Such documents should include birth certificates, marriage certificate, insurance policies, medical records, school records, drivers licence, car insurance, pharmacy records, and lists of important names, addresses and phone numbers, including solicitors, citizens' advice centres and welfare offices. A visit to the citizens' advice centre could also be made prior to fleeing. They will give you advice and relevant addresses and phone numbers. Since it is likely that you have been isolated during the abusive tenure, try to build up as much support as possible prior to leaving. This includes not only professional support mentioned here, but also reconnecting with friends, family and relatives.

Buying a mobile (cell) phone to maintain contact is also important. This will allow you to communicate with relevant people such as your children's school, the police, neighbours, friends, or any helpful persons. My advice would be not to make such phone contact until you are far away from the abusive home.

The survival kit should also include essential items purchased from the domestic finances prior to departure. Such items would include extra clothing and sufficient medicines.

Finally, you might like to make arrangements for your children's pets, if any. It is traumatic for children to leave their pets, and it might be possible to take small pets with you. If not, you might wish to leave them with a willing friend. You will know what to do.

I hope that this short chapter will give you relevant ideas, and help you make the difficult decision to leave an abusive environment. Take heart from Linda's words, as she came to grips with, and overcame, her feelings about the 'stigma' of her marriage breakdown.

> I have also learned not to take on board opinions people have towards me that are not in a good nature. Even though we live in 2010, there is a certain stigma when a marriage breaks down. When you say to people that you are separated, some feel uncomfortable straight away. You can feel this in the conversation. Not everyone is like this, of course, but many people are.
>
> I have neighbours near my home who gave me THAT look – the kind of look where you know they are saying, 'She's broken up with her husband'. I have one neighbour who will no longer say hello to me since my marriage has broken down.
>
> This is just another side effect of a marriage breakdown; I used to find this hard at the start and felt embarrassed if someone that felt this way toward marriage breakdown saw me. I would nearly hide, so I wouldn't get the look of distaste. But over time, it does get somewhat easier. I tell it as it is now. I am separated and I am a single mother. I don't hide if from people I know and people I meet. This is my life, and if they feel awkward being around me because of that – that's their problem!

Chapter 11

What Happens after Leaving
an Abusive Relationship?

Take my hands, my children,
And look into the sun,
We will create our world,
Unwatched and unfettered.
The light shines through the trees,
As they green in time of spring.
I see the summer in your eyes,
Clouded by the storms of winter.
The winter clouds view the horizon,
Driven by the icy wind that chills the soul.
The gentle breeze of Spring rescues you
From barren waste
And I will hold you, too
In loving embrace,
And look into the future
Mirrored in your hopeful face.

Jim O'Shea

It is difficult to imagine the emotional turmoil that victims feel when they leave an abusive relationship. Linda gives us some idea of what it is like.

Your feelings when you leave can be scary, because they make no sense. It is just a big whirlwind, and you are just swished around in this whirlwind, with no control. I felt every emotion I can think of – sadness, anger, helplessness, loss, loneliness, stress, pain, unhappiness with the world, shock, no understanding of my life, loss of hope for me and my life, confusion and anxiety. Some days I would wake up so sad, and had no interest in the day. Then it could turn to anger and I would say, 'No! I'm not giving up. I am going to make a life for me and my son'. Every day would bring such a mixture of emotions and feelings; it was so hard to keep in line with everyday life, like going to work.

Stress was a huge factor for me. I had been left with such a mess on top of my marriage failure. I was left with such financial burdens, and a completely new life to build. I was getting threatening letters every day from banks. It was just one thing after another. I could go to work, sad from the loss of the relationship. Then it could turn to anger so quickly, when I would come home and see all these letters and all the problems he had left me to sort out, as he walked away. Confusion is such a big part of things, too. It's impossible to rationalise any of what is going on in your life. How you got to this stage, and how it went so wrong.

Then you ask yourself the question, was part of it your fault? Why has he such hate and anger in him? Were you doing something wrong that he was so unhappy? And why wasn't he happy and content with what he had, as you were, and as you both were when you met? It's impossible to answer all the questions that go around and around in your head.

Of course, there is the stage where you long for your partner and dwell on all the good times. I think I spent a lot of time on my own thinking about this. But when I would get really sad about the marriage ending, I would pick up the phone and talk to friends and family, and they would give me the courage, or that little shove that I would need to pick myself up and keep going!

Sometimes I would be paranoid that he might come to the house during the middle of the night in a rage before he left the country, and so all doors from most rooms were locked. I used to lock my bedroom door, and for a while I slept with either a hurley or hockey stick by my locker, in case I was put in the position that I had to protect me and my child from him.

Despite the trepidation, the questions and the fear that you feel, you will survive the abuse, recover and re-experience independence, happiness and peace. Part of our work as humans is to integrate our suffering, as we strive for happiness. We have the capacity, irrespective of apparently insurmountable obstacles, to create a life where we can grow, reach our potential, and experience joy. It is a fundamental principle that we have within ourselves everything we need to be happy, including the capacity to recover. However, it may take a long time for your scars to heal. It may take years before you trust again. Even when you meet a non-abusive partner, you will be on the alert, always waiting for an attack. Learning to trust and experience non-judgemental love within a new relationship is one of the best antidotes to the after-effects of an abusive relationship. Gradually the feeling of wariness will abate. Initially, you might be better to focus on social relationships rather than intimate ones, because this provides a safer context to rebuild relational skills.

When you leave an abusive relationship, you are no longer a victim, but a survivor. The stench of the abuse may linger for a long time, and you may be confused by the loving feelings and longing you experience for the nice Jekyll, before you begin to confront the vicious Hyde, and you may, perhaps, experience bitterness and regret. But as you slowly find your feet in the new space you have created, you will begin to see possibilities, and enter the recovery stage, where you will enhance your life and be as you want to be. As you had the strength to endure the abusive relationship, and to leave it, you also have the strength to create a new life. It takes time, and there will be setbacks, as you set about recovering your optimism and reclaiming your identity.

Initially you needed to create a safety plan to make the world a more secure place. Previously you lived in an unsafe place, and now you bring about a physical and psychological distance from the abuser, to reclaim yourself, regain your power and identity, and dispel the confusion created by years of abuse. Sometimes it can take a long time to ensure a safe world. Some of the appendices in the 2010 report by Cosc, outlining the national strategy on domestic, sexual and gender-based violence, lists many organisations where you will find appropriate support. You can get this report in your local library. This would also be relevant to the immediate period when you are planning to escape from your abusive environment. The Mid-West Region of the HSE has a very valuable information document that lists various support agencies for the region. I imagine that all the other regions have a similar resource. It is no bigger than a banking card.

A vital element of your survival plan will involve having a good therapist, GP, and family law solicitor. Such professional support will increase your sense of power and help you deal with isolation, one of the main obstacles to survival. When you were abused, you were isolated and silenced. Now you have to undo this conditioning, and realise that not all relationships are abusive or sexual. You will free yourself from this shackle, and reach out to others. This positive coping strategy helps to reduce anxiety in the immediate term, and expel it in the long term. Re-establishing contact with friends and making new friends not only counteracts this anxiety and worry but also adds to the safety of your new home. You may find, however, that some erstwhile friends may be uncomfortable, for various reasons, with a separated person. It can also be distressing to find that abusers may get more loyalty and sympathy from some others, because they have more contact with them. Abusers sometimes gain sympathy by portraying themselves as the innocent victims of separation, as they bluntly deny any abuse. Thus, they hope to enlist the help of others in condemning survivors and keeping them isolated. They wish to destabilise the survivors and prevent them from moving on. Linda was fortunate, however, and managed to reconnect with erstwhile friends, who rallied to her. It is clear that they liked her, and missed her when she became isolated from them through the control exercised by her abusive husband.

I have made an effort to take up all my friendships, including some of the closest ones that I had with my cousins. It felt great to get back in contact with them. However, some contacts did take a lot of work, as I had hurt people with the way I just walked out of their lives. I even organised a college reunion last year, and caught up with all of my college class. It felt so good to be able to meet up with them, without being made feel guilty. They are all good friends, and I shouldn't have been made feel guilty about talking to them, whether they were male or female. We are all in touch now via email or on the net, and it's great. I am so delighted that I did it. My friends told me that they felt uncomfortable around Stephen. Of course they did. If I could feel the tension around him when I was out with him, they could too. At the time, I was so busy trying to calm him to make sure that he did not boil over, and hit one, that I didn't even notice that they could see through it all.

She was also fortunate in that she had never lost contact with her parents. Her father was particularly supportive.

My father came to me one day and said that he had got an interview for me with his colleague in my hometown, if I was interested. I look back now and I think that maybe my dad was planning a future for my son and me. Maybe he could see what was going to happen. I wasn't sure, because it would involve commuting. On the other hand, I would be around people in my hometown, instead of living in an isolated area, not knowing anyone. So I went for my interview and I got it. My mother had a local child-minder sorted out within a few days near my home. Everything fell into place very quickly. Maybe it was fate. I think my angels helped me to be some way prepared for what was to come. I was happy in this job and could call home and stay a night or so when I wanted to do that. I was quite happy. If only my marriage had been so happy.

As Linda shows, leaving an abusive relationship can be traumatic, and the abuser may resort to all sorts of controlling behaviours to torment you, and re-establish power over you. It is, therefore, not always easy to ensure protection. The first step is to establish physical boundaries. This means getting as far away as you can. It also means having as little contact with the abuser as possible.

There are other practical steps you can take to maximise safety, although some of these are more feasible in cities. Renting a post office box or using the address of a friend for mail is one suggestion. It is always important to hide the new address from the abuser, so only close friends should know it. I would suggest changing the number of a mobile phone, and having it cloaked. The phone company could also issue a caller ID facility on your phone, and your landline could be blocked and unlisted. Children also need protection, and so school authorities should be alerted to the situation. If you have moved a long distance you will have changed your children's school, and the head teacher should be advised of the situation. Alert neighbours, and ask that they contact the police if there is the possibility of danger. A motion-sensitive lighting system is somewhat of a deterrent, and could be part of the overall strategy to prevent contact with the abuser. Of course, he may have rights of visitation to the children, and in such cases some of the above suggestions are not relevant. However, if you feel that the children are again at risk, you can take steps to have such rights withdrawn.

Irrespective of the measures you take, your erstwhile abuser may use unscrupulous methods in his desire to keep control over you. He may refuse to contribute any maintenance for the children's support, and use the children in other ways to distress a mother already worried about the possible destructive impact of the abuse on them. Some abusive fathers, who have every right of access, may use them to undermine their mother. They use them to get information about her, neglect them when they stay with him, try to divide them from her, threaten to take them from her, seek increased custody, and generally make every effort to disrupt the family. Female abusers resort to similar tactics.

One of the most malignant post-separation control methods is stalking and harassing the survivor. Stalking is illegal in most developed countries, and is a pattern of behaviour with intent to instil fear. It often goes on for several years and it can demoralise you and make your life a misery.It is an obsessive behaviour and therefore very dangerous. The stalker usually starts with annoying, obscene or threatening phone calls, and follows this up with visits to the home or the workplace of the survivor. Stalkers often carry out acts of violence aimed at the survivors' property, pets and even at the survivors themselves. Again, they may use the children for this end. There are many examples of abusers frightening the children, threatening them, harming them, and even kidnapping them. Your one-time abuser may also attend sporting events in which your children are involved and sit near you to intimidate you. You may also find him sitting next to you if you are having a meal in a restaurant. No place is sacrosanct to the abuser.

Cyber stalking is especially destabilising. Instances have arisen of stalkers concealing GPS equipment in the survivor's car to track her movements. You should also be aware that computers might be used to gather information about you. Some survivors turn to chat rooms for support and advice. It is easy for an abuser to pose as a supportive female, make contact with the survivor, and gather information. This further feeds their jealousy and need for control.

Yet you are not without power when dealing with stalking and harassment. On a psychological level, it is best not to react, because any reaction gives the abuser satisfaction and encourages him in his behaviour. Personal power can best be maintained by creating psychological boundaries, which means being aware of the buttons that abusers can push, and disconnecting from them. Controlling or concealing anger, resentment and bitterness deprives the stalker of the satisfaction of witnessing the torment of the survivor, and may help to weaken his resolve to pursue. On a practical level, stalking should be reported to the police, although this is not very effective. After all, a person is entitled to attend events in which their children are taking part. Nevertheless, research shows that being confronted by a police officer can deter some abusers. If you wish to take legal action at some stage, you should keep a diary of all stalking events. There is nothing as powerful as a written record, because it may show a pattern. If the stalker makes phone threats, it might be possible to record them also.

As well as a safety plan, you should also have an uncomplicated survival/recovery plan. A safety plan means external safety, a survival/recovery plan means having a measure of internal security. When you consider the debilitating effects of abuse, and how you are almost owned by the perpetrators, you probably realise how difficult it can be to feel secure within. Remember you have a great number of unrecognised resources. Set achievable goals for your recovery, otherwise the victim's self-critical tendency will set in and you will be tormented by self-blame for failing to successfully complete your plan. Be gentle with yourself, accept yourself, and try not to blame yourself for the breakdown of your relationship. You must begin to nurture yourself to counteract being emotionally famished by your abuser.

Caring for yourself and treating yourself with tenderness will have a healing effect, and will help raise your self-esteem. When I was in training, some of my colleagues often told me I was self-judgemental and hard on myself. My experience has been that although I have come to love myself, both the good and the shadow side, it has been a long process, and I still can be hard on myself. Very often we need someone to remind us of how harsh we are on ourselves.

The importance of self-care and basic health cannot be over-emphasised as part of the survival/recovery plan. The Hidden Hurt website (www.hiddenhurt.co.uk), which is worth visiting, outlines four areas of self-care (physical, psychological, emotional and spiritual), which would be helpful following a separation. Physical self-care includes regular and healthy eating, plenty of exercise, medical care, sufficient sleep, vacations, and having time alone. Psychological self-care involves therapy, light reading, reflecting, getting involved in new activities, and paying attention to your thoughts, beliefs and attitudes. Any material on awareness, such as books or CDs, will help. It is also psychologically beneficial to personalise your new environment, making it a familiar place with your identity on it. Paint a room, put up new pictures, and so on.

I think that the creative use of a journal is also a powerful psychological aid to self-care. It can be your 'creative journal' for your art, poetry and narrative. I used poetry when I was going through bereavement following the death of my child. You do not have to be a good poet or a good artist. The process is the important thing. Linda found that writing her story, which is a more expanded use of a journal, was one of the most beneficial factors in her recovery. As she compiled it she came to see Stephen's pattern of abusive behaviour, and while not obliterating the kind Jekyll, she got a clearer image of the malign Hyde in this powerful passage. As you will see later, Linda's image of Hyde was not as clear as she thought at this stage. But this is how she felt and thought at that stage, when Stephen was still in Canada.

> Writing this story has brought me on such a memory trip. I feel like I have been on a long journey of my life. It was very hard emotionally as I was writing and remembering details of events, and the hurtful things that have happened. But, more importantly, writing my story has helped me so much. Each time I wrote an episode of something that had happened, I felt the emotion and pain, and I cried it out. I also, however, began to see, as I put what happened in black and white, just how much my husband had done to me; just how much I was in his web of betrayal, pain, anger, hurt. A web of no love. None whatsoever. I may have loved him, but I was just foolish

thinking that he loved me or ever would. He is not able to love anyone. When I started my counselling and this story, I often wondered would he change. Maybe someday he would knock on my door and be a different man. Now I accept that that is very unlikely to happen. And more importantly, if he did knock on my door and claimed he was a new man, I wouldn't care. It is only from telling my story from the magical relationship that it started off to be to where I am now that I realise there is no room for this man in my heart. He cannot give me the love and caring that I deserve, or the life that I want for my son. Since writing this story, I have learned about his control and I have identified in writing this story how he used it. He was using his control within the relationship even at early stages, but I couldn't see it.

I now know how not to fall into his control traps. I have also begun to realise how far I have come. My son and I have built a good life, one that I am very comfortable and happy with. I found writing the story a great release, or a great way of dealing with everything I was going through. It has really opened my eyes to the horrible, ugly side of this relationship. Before counselling and this book, the good charming side that was at the beginning of our relationship kept overshadowing the ugly side. Now the ugly side shows its face in a clear picture to me!

Emotional self-care entails being with people you like and enjoy, praising and affirming yourself, playing with children, looking at comedies, and allowing your feelings. Spiritual self-care is about spending time with nature, being open to inspiration, cherishing optimism and hope, meditating, praying, singing, feeling awe, and reading inspirational literature. Her faith was especially important in helping Linda to survive the early days of separation.

I constantly prayed to the angels for guidance and courage. When I wasn't sure of where things were going, or what was to be my next move, I would pray to them and ask for guidance. I found it a tremendous comfort to know that they are always with me, and that they are always there to help. They never let me down. They helped me on dark nights, when I would be trying to go asleep – when my mind was restless, and thoughts were whizzing around my head, thoughts of everything, my husband who was gone, the dream I had lost, the home and life I knew were gone, how would my son react to the fact his father isn't in his life, and lots of other things. I prayed to my angels and asked for peace, so I could get some badly needed rest. I have yet to find a night when this prayer for peace in my mind wasn't answered.

Sometimes on my lunch break, when I was struggling, and finding it hard to cope and trying to fight back tears, I would go to my local church, and sit there and talk to God. I felt at peace and felt such calmness in the church – it was like a hideaway from the rest of the world. To me it allowed me to run away from the outside world that was pulling me in all directions, and just let me sit in peace and calm, and relax, and pray for help and guidance. I used to pray for my husband too, that God would help him throughout life, and maybe help him see the hurt and pain he is causing, and to help him become a better father.

If possible, your survival/recovery plan should include having therapy. It takes courage to enter therapy. Talking to a stranger about intimate and shameful matters is not easy. And this stranger is in a position of power. As a survivor, you know what it is like to have your power taken away, and it is right to be cautious and even suspicious as you enter therapy. It is, however, important to choose a therapist who is right for you. Specific therapies will be necessary for victims who experienced serious sexual assault, who have become addicted to a substance or to self-mutilation. It is really important in therapy not to be re-traumatised, and so it is vital to choose a therapist well trained in dealing with abuse and trauma, where you can safely vent your feelings, get suggestions, and bring your resources into awareness. This is akin to being 'built up' psychologically to take the hard road of exploring your life as an abuse victim.

You can only do this if you have a good connection with your therapist, otherwise move on to another therapist after a few sessions.

In the safe setting of counselling, you should be able to safely deal with the emotional impact of the abuse, and with thinking distortions, behavioural patterns, the spiritual losses, and loss in general. Feelings of shame, worthlessness, power-lessness, confusion, fear, and so on must be explored. The confusion that abuse engenders must be teased out and disentangled, and the possible existence of a codependent personality. The counsellor will check if survivors are using negative coping mechanisms which work in the short term but in the long term are harmful and prevent healing. Such nega-tive activities include smoking, taking drugs, cutting themselves off from other people, workaholism, violent behav-iour, unhealthy eating, and self-destructive behaviour such as self-harming or suicide attempts.

For a time, Linda struggled on without counselling, but she needed help in exploring her pain and confusion, and found the experience to be

> ... one of the best decisions for me and really brought me along the road of recovery. I have peace in my mind now, and can go to bed in peace and sleep without horrible dreams, a thing I often wondered if I ever would have again.

She reveals how counselling helped her, and hopefully will help you, as you set about rebuilding your new life.

> Counselling has helped me enormously. It has helped me understand. It has also helped me to accept things as they are, and to accept my feelings as they come to me. I always tried to fight any feelings of sadness toward my ex husband. When I cried, I used to say to myself 'don't be so stupid – why are you crying over someone that had done all this to you and doesn't care one bit – you are so stupid and pathetic'. And so I would hold back my tears.

Now I have learned that it's ok to cry over him. It's a feeling, and there is nothing wrong with that. I have learned to accept all my feelings as they come to me, whether it is anger, hate, longing for our past life, love, sadness or whatever feeling comes along.

I've also learned to understand how abusers work. Stephen used always turn things back on me for things he would do, and he was so cunning he would have me questioning myself, saying, 'am I the one with the problem? Have I issues? Am I not well like he says?' Now I have learned that I am not the abuser here. I am the survivor. I did not cause him to be abusive. He chose those actions. He chose his behaviour, not me. I am not responsible for his behaviour or happiness. He is.

I've learned that it is up to individuals themselves to be happy. No one else can make them happy. I also learned more about boundaries, something that I didn't have within my marriage. I had no boundaries. When I first attended counselling there was so much going on in my mind, and I was so confused. My emotions were all over the place, and I was trying to fight them. My thoughts were everywhere. I was so confused. By going to counselling, I let all the hurt and pain come out, as I went back in my mind to everything that happened. Yes, it was so painful, and I grieved, and I am still grieving over the loss. But I have more of an understanding and acceptance of things now.

I have talked through all my thoughts and worries. And it is such a release to get them all out in the open to a non-judgemental person. I needed to get all of it out. It was all stored in my head and was going around and around and getting nowhere. It was like a big whirlwind of thoughts and worries that were not being solved, and were going nowhere.

I have mentioned in the previous chapter that people have remained in abusive relationships because they have failed to grieve their losses. This grieving process will now be part of your survival/recovery plan, and the help of a counsellor is advisable in this. Remember that while Linda understands the dynamic of abuse, she still has to deal with her feelings. Understanding is only part of grieving. Firstly, you mourn the loss of the nice Jekyll and all his admirable qualities. You grieve the loss of this charming companion and the warmth and love he initially brought to the relationship. When Linda first came to me she could not understand why she still had feelings for her abusive husband. Her friends frequently challenged her about having loving feelings for this abuser. But the following extract from her story about the early days of her marriage shows why these feelings persisted.

> I lived my life with Stephen happily. He was so caring toward me. Even if I had a slight pain in my stomach, he would be so attentive to me and would say things like 'I hate seeing you like this.' I only had a sore stomach, but I found him so caring and used to think how nice this was to have such a sensitive man, a man that cared and loved me so much. I used always see a bright future for us. I knew I wanted him in my life and that we could have a happy life together. A life full of love and passion, just as it was all the time with us. He used to tell me all the time that he loved me, and that I was everything to him, and how happy he was that I was in his life, and that he had met me. He used to say things like 'look at how much we accomplish together', i.e. buying the house and starting a new, exciting life in Galway.

You, too, may have to grieve the loss of a caring partner, and you move on to mourn the loss of self-esteem, of personal integrity, of relationship, of intimacy, of friends, of control, of safety, of personal meaning, of a father/mother to your children. You mourn the loss of your dreams, your hopes, your future without your partner, and the possible lack of closure. Your therapist will help you explore the story of your relationship, and you will come to identify your particular losses.

Bereavement theorists offer several frameworks to help us grieve. William Worden, one of the great experts on grief, tells us that we have four tasks to perform to successfully mourn a loss.

We must first accept the reality of the permanent loss of the relationship. In parts of her narrative, Linda believed that she had reached this stage, and did not regret making every effort to save the marriage, including her decision to return.

> I criticised myself that night so much for giving him another chance, and that when I left for those few months at my parents' house, I should have stayed gone. But looking back now, I'm glad I gave us another chance, because I put my heart and soul into us, and he walked all over it. And now I can look back and say I gave it my best shot, and I had to do this for myself, so that I wouldn't feel guilty about leaving, and bringing my son with me and letting him be from a broken home. This hurt so much! Of course, this wasn't the only reason for leaving, as explained earlier, but it definitely gave me that nudge that I needed to get out. I realised that night that Jack and I didn't matter to him anymore.

There can be several false endings when the survivor returns to the relationship, and this makes it difficult to acknowledge the real ending when it comes. It also involves recognising that you never really knew the abusive partner, but loved an idealised or non-existent person.

Secondly, we must work through the pain of the grief, which will involve many feelings such as anger, guilt, loneliness, depression, sadness and longing. You feel anger at the Hyde and longing for the Jekyll. You may be filled with confusion at these contradictory feelings, but ultimately you will get perspective on the relationship. This can be painful and challenging.

Your third task is to adjust to your new world in which your partner is missing. Remember that despite the obstacles you face, you are the creator of this new world. Your abusive partner is no longer with you and your central question is 'who am I now?' You redefine yourself, find meaning in the loss, regain control, and begin to see the world as a benevolent place. Elaine Weiss has some good examples of women empowering themselves having escaped the clutches of abusive partners. One woman quickly reclaimed her maiden name, and this became a symbol of obliterating her marriage; for example, whenever she found a document with her married name on it, she covered it over using markers. Perhaps 'obliterating' the marriage may be an unfortunate term, because you must integrate it as part of your life experience. As Linda surveyed the wreckage of her marriage, she saw her new life as being free of her abusive husband.

> Stephen hasn't been a husband to me for such a long time, I feel he doesn't deserve the title 'my husband', because when I think of this title I think of someone that will love, care and protect me, and he provides none of these. I don't want to be referred to as his wife anymore, I am not his wife in my eyes. We haven't seen each other for over a year, and we have no contact. He does nothing to help with his son, or with anything. I want to be free from him.

Neither was she willing to celebrate the end of her relationship.

> A lot of friends have said to me, 'we will celebrate that day when you are granted your separation from him. We will organise dinner and drinks to celebrate'. But what is there really to celebrate? This day will be the end of so much – a marriage I had such dreams for, a chapter in my life that I gave my heart and soul for, the family unit, even though it is gone a long time, my title as Stephen's wife – the title I was proud and happy to take on the day we got married. I think this day in court is a sad day, and it is a sad day for any couple who have to go to this stage. Remember the day the marriage was made, we celebrated it with friends and family. It was a day of happiness and joy, and now we end it in so official a way, in a courtroom with a group of professional strangers,

who don't know either one of us. How can this be a day
to celebrate?

She also recognised that they had happy times, and she was
determined that these would be preserved, so she kept some
photos and her wedding album when she left Stephen. I feel
that she was steadily gaining a very healthy and balanced
psychological state of mind.

> The reason I brought the album and video is that I knew
> he would destroy them in his rage. Despite the pain and
> hurt the breakdown of our marriage had brought us, I
> was the happiest woman on this planet the day I married
> him. My wedding day memories are something no one
> can take away from me. It is a part of my life, and I want
> to be able to hold onto that day. Even though the
> marriage is over now, that good day and the good parts
> of our relationship I am glad and grateful to have experi-
> enced. They were such happy days. I hope one day I
> might be able to look at the wedding album or video as it
> is a part of my life and me. The marriage may be over, but
> the memories last, both good and bad, and both are part
> of my life, so I'm not going to try to wipe any of them
> clear from my life. I just want to be able one day to accept
> both memories calmly without being upset, and get on
> and live some more good memories.

Your fourth task is to emotionally relocate the lost partner
and move on. You will reconcile conflicting emotions, realise
that you will not forget the relationship experience, good and
bad, and experience the relief of leaving an abusive environment and travelling the road to peace and, hopefully, love.
Many of Elaine Weiss's narrators eventually learned to trust,
and to take the risk of a new relationship. Educating yourself
on the nature of abuse and abusers will make it a little easier
for you to make a better choice of partner. Most of her narrators had better luck second time round.

It is vital to complete the grieving stages or grieving tasks.
Sometimes you may be disappointed and shocked when you

feel that you have succeeded and are ready to move on and your feelings for your partner return with even greater intensity. This may happen when a partner emigrates and returns. In the meantime the survivor goes through what he or she thinks is the entire process of grieving. Linda's story in the above paragraphs indicates that she felt she was ready to move on. But when Stephen suddenly returned from Canada, she unexpectedly found herself overwhelmed with conflicting emotions, and returned to counselling to deal with this crisis. She successfully met this challenge in the short space of ten weeks. Basically, she had moved a long way down the road of grieving, but she had not reached the end of that road. Do not be surprised if that happens to you.

When Stephen rang to say that he was returning, Linda initially felt a plethora of negative emotions. She felt angry, suspicious, mistrustful, and concerned about the possible impact on her child. How would Jack respond to his father? Would Stephen befriend him and abandon him again? The peace she had so painfully achieved was shattered and her emotional turmoil increased on the Sunday they had agreed to meet.

> I was upside down with emotions. I was angry, anxious, stressed and upset. It had been so long, I didn't know how to be. We pulled up in our car, and waited. He arrived. I introduced Jack, who hid behind my legs for a while, but eventually he came around. They played and they seemed to do very well. It was so strange, though, after all this time. He told me about his experiences of his travelling. He was nice and very warm with his personality. He said that he had changed, and had learned so much from his travels that he wants to make things better.
>
> He met Jack on a number of occasions; I always accompanied my child because I didn't want to leave him on his own with him. I had very little trust in him. I waited to see when he would get tired of handing over money for Jack, and spending time with him on Sundays. But he didn't

break any of his promises, and was there when he was meant to be.

Despite her initial reservation, Linda found herself being drawn into the web again.

In the meantime, my mind was playing havoc along with my feelings. I was beginning to ponder over the thought 'had he changed?' and had life experiences in travelling changed his perception on things, that maybe he can see the damage he had done.

It wasn't long before he was asking for us to give things a go again. He promised all the good things, pleaded that we should be a family again, and not to keep the family apart. That he has changed now, and is ready for a family and for settling down. He told me he still loved me and always would. He said we would have back what we once had.

Deep down I knew none of this would happen and that this was a big fantasy. I have learned so much about abuse that I knew this was the NICE Stephen coming forth and the ugly one was to follow. However, this didn't prevent havoc on my emotions and feelings. It was as if all the pain and hurt and loss was brought to the surface again. When I had seen Stephen for the first time with our son, it immediately brought it to the surface like a volcano erupting. Once again I found myself in pain! How could this happen? I thought I had dealt with all of this. I couldn't believe it was happening again.

Stephen's return had reopened my grief – every inch of the pain and hurt, sorrow, loneliness, stress and longing for when it was good. I soon realised that I WAS STILL GRIEVING MY MARRIAGE. Stephen in reality in front of me brought all that back to me. I went over the marriage again and again. I took out the photos of the wedding day and cried. I cried looking at my son asleep, longing for the dreams that were in place for our family, before it was ripped apart.

I shut everyone out, I went to work and when I came home I shut the door and wanted to hide from the world.

I looked forward to going to sleep at night because it would give me peace for a few hours from the world and my pain. Because no one would understand how I could be upset. He had left for so long and done so much – how could I still be upset? But, these were my feelings and I couldn't prevent them. I knew I had to accept them and take the time to myself to deal with it all, and go through all the feelings that had once again resurfaced.

Meanwhile, Stephen was trying his utmost for me to give him a chance and go back. The strength I had to gain to do this was very hard. On one occasion, Stephen brushed his hand on my back. This might seem like an insignificant thing to do, but in the light of what I was going through it was hugely emotional. I knew that this was going too far, and was too dangerous. I was on very thin ice. I knew very clearly that Stephen didn't love me, that he was not going to be there for me and Jack.

So I understood the reality, but my feelings played havoc in my fantasy world of what it could be like to be back as a family again.

I was surprised when Linda returned for counselling. From her previous narrative and the exploration of her issues I wrongly assumed that she had completed her grieving, and would be able to withstand any emotional impact his eventual return would have on her. But when grieving is incomplete, returning feelings can be overwhelming. It is like the final sting of a dying wasp. Therapy, therefore, is important to embrace and complete the journey of grief. If therapy is too expensive for you as a way of grieving and exploring the dynamics of your abusive relationship, there are other ways that you can cope, integrate and eventually grow. It is always beneficial to talk to other survivors, and perhaps join a support group, although Mike Lew advises that it is best to see a therapist for a while before joining a group. Group work will help you to feel less alone, to feel understood, or perhaps to receive practical help, especially if you suffer from Post Traumatic Stress Disorder. Victims of abuse lose a sense of identity, and often become disconnected and split within themselves, so volunteer work in the community can reconnect you with other people, and help you reclaim your sense of worth. You will receive assistance from the state body, the HSE, and support from some of the voluntary organisations mentioned in the next chapter.

There are many relaxation techniques that you might find useful. These include breathing exercises, stretching, meditation, yoga, guided meditation, mindfulness, prayer, listening to quiet music, and walking in a rural area. I often suggest to distressed people to create a personal space, where they can listen to soft music, light candles and have a small indoor water feature. It will be their soothing haven. However, soothing exercises must be managed carefully, because when a survivor is relaxed, the intrusive thoughts of the abuse may intrude. Apart from relaxation, there are positive distracting activities to help alleviate the after-effects of trauma; for example, an exercise programme would include walking, swimming, jogging, and perhaps gym activity.

Ultimately, some people may wish to confront the abuser as an aid to recovery. Survivors will make up their own minds about the feasibility and safety of such a course. Confrontation gives back power and gives a voice, but caution is advised. It should not be hasty, but should be planned. I believe that the best place to lay out a plan is with the help of a therapist, or a reliable friend. It is advisable to consider the pros and cons of confrontation, talk to others about their experiences on confrontation, and to those who decided not to confront. Write down what you would like to say, and discuss it with your counsellor. Perhaps some role-play in the safety of the counsellor's room might help. Role-play can make the confrontation much more realistic, and help you to assess if you are psychologically ready for it. If you decide to go ahead and confront the perpetrator, make sure the meeting place is safe. Finally, be aware that the result of the confrontation may not be as you hoped. It is likely that the perpetrator will deny, be vague, or minimise the abuse. But, in a sense, you do not need validation of the abuse. You know it happened. Remember, no matter what the result, your action is for yourself, and it reinforces your courage and your emergence from the shadow of the abuser. Mic Hunter makes the useful point that the work in the preparation to confront has greater healing than the actual confrontation.

There are, of course, other ways of confrontation, such as sending a letter or prosecuting the criminal. If he or she is dead, you could also write the unsent letter. As you saw in Anna's case in the context of workplace abuse, it is a powerful way of getting your feelings out and flexing your emotional muscles. It is advisable to write these in the safety of the counselling room, because they inevitably bring up strong emotions.

As you work your way through your losses, you may also be engaging in the process of legal separation, and counselling will help you make that sometimes long and painful journey. But despite the reservations already made about the legal process, you will require the assistance of a good family law solicitor. You have left the abusive relationship and now face the prospect of a long and difficult legal journey. The story of Linda and the legal process might help you to understand the emotional rollercoaster that you may experience as you travel that road. She is lucky because she found a supportive solicitor, and did not incur much expense because she has free legal aid. She found it a relief that the solicitor would deal will all matters relating to the separation, including the financial mess left by Stephen. However, she is concerned about appearing in court where she will have to endure having their personal details aired. As it happened, Stephen did not return from Canada to attend court, and Linda was granted a separation and full custody. This meant that he could only see Jack under Linda's supervision. This was always her wish, and she adhered strictly to it.

You might, however, like to know how Linda felt prior to the court hearing, not knowing that Stephen would remain in

Canada and not having any legal representation in court. Her thoughts and feelings might reflect some of yours.

> It is a day I wait in anticipation for, and is a day I will be anxious and worried about until it is over. Each day I try to put it to the back of my mind. I find I get so tired spinning round and round in my head what is going to be said, or what might happen on the day. It is so stressful. It is also hard to contemplate that one day can make such life-changing decisions. Everything is very hazy now. I also don't know what his plan is for the day in court. I am unsure as to whether he will turn up in court on the day. This is one of my biggest fears. I haven't seen him for so long, I don't know how I will react. I know, however, that if he turns up, it will open up an emotional rollercoaster in me. I haven't seen this man for so long, yet he has such an impact on my life in negative ways. I am afraid when I see him that the emotional feelings of the nice Stephen will arise. The good times always come into my head, but I have to say over time it is getting easier to deal with them. This is because I am getting more understanding of the way Stephen is, and why he turned from a lovely caring man to someone completely different. But on this day I have to stay strong. I can't let the emotional part of all of this take me over. I need to keep my strength and wits about me, so that I can work at getting what is fair, and what my son and I deserve from this separation.

We have seen in the last chapter that fear of not having sufficient access sometimes keeps victims in an abusive relationship. When one leaves this may become a reality, and may generate conflict and anger. Separated fathers are often distraught, because they have insufficient time to see their children, perhaps because a controlling ex-wife wishes to punish them by denying them enough access. However, some parents fear for the emotional well being of their children if the ex-partner has been abusive in the relationship. That was Linda's great fear.

Access is going to be an issue on this day, and I am worried about this. My son doesn't know his dad. This is such a sad statement, but it is fact. Jack doesn't know what a dad is. I am not sure what memories, if any at all, he has of him. He hasn't seen him in well over a year. And he has grown and advanced so much in that space of time that he is no longer a toddler, but a boy. I worry about the fact that his father doesn't live in this country, and has mentioned that he wants access when he can get home. But how will that work for Jack? His dad will come into his life, introduce himself as his dad, and then leave and go back to his other life. No one will know when he will come home again, and in the meantime I am left to pick up the pieces, as the little boy is left wondering where daddy is gone, and when he will see him again. I don't want my son hurt or emotionally damaged over this, and am adamant that if access is wanted, it needs to be regular and supervised for the foreseeable future. I really worry about Stephen gaining access without supervision. The last time he took him, he dropped him back home in the car with no child seat. This is so dangerous. I don't want my son subjected to this kind of danger. I am so mad at Stephen for all this; I hate him for being so selfish. When does he ever think of Jack? Never! It is always about what he wants or feels, never what his son might need, or want, or feel.

Fortunately, as stated, she now has sole control, and Stephen's irregular visits do not seem to have a negative impact on Jack. The child never bonded with his father, and is too young to miss him. Linda worries, however, that when Jack reaches teenage years he may blame her, believing, perhaps, that she had kept him from his father. In reality, and despite her reservations about Stephen, Linda feels that her child should meet his father. It may be painful for her at times, but she puts her child's needs first. Her close supervision of their encounters eases her mind that her child may suffer some emotional damage from contact with his abusive father.

Distress is also caused by some abusive partners manipulating the legal process as a means of control over the survivor. Some make excuses to postpone court hearings as a way to control. At one stage, Linda worried that Stephen would use his absence from Ireland as a means of delaying the separation process. The process was somewhat delayed, but the judge quickly realised the true situation, and, to her relief, the process was successfully concluded. The following part of her narrative shows her fear during the waiting period.

> Stephen has used any step he can to drag out the separation, from not providing a forwarding address in Canada to having post refused at his parents' house. It has been a long drawn out process. It is so frustrating, and just when I think it is moving along, he does something to slow it down. I tried to locate an address from one of his family members, where we could issue papers, as Stephen would not provide an address. After going through all that hassle and giving him plenty of time, he didn't respond. Then after a number of weeks, when it suited him, he hired a solicitor to represent him from Canada. But because of the fact that he is in another country with different time zones, it's hard for my solicitor to make contact. At the moment, we are not sure if an Irish solicitor will be appointed, or what is the plan. Because of the fact that he is now so far away he is entitled to more time to get paperwork sorted out, once again slowing up the whole process. Even though I started the legal separation, he seems to have gained control of the whole process, and once again, everyone is moving to his terms. I feel that it is so unfair.

It *was* unfair. It was a bullying tactic. It was also bluff. Stephen did not have the money to pay a solicitor. His profligate ways continued in Canada.

It was a relief for Linda when the separation order was granted, and on her desired terms. I have no doubt that she has now completed her counselling, and can look forward and move on. Ultimately, too, your counselling will end, and the legal process will be completed. During this time, you will have done your best to practise self-care and keep you and your children safe. You slowly build a new life and new relationships, and if your circumstances allow, you may begin to think about forgiveness. Some survivors tell me that it is the greatest healer of all, and they want to know how to reach it. I do not have the answer. Some of the survivors who told their stories to Elaine Weiss managed to forgive their abusive partners. However, you cannot force yourself to forgive. Sometimes it arrives apparently unexpectedly. However, if it happens, it can only do so after the long road of rehabilitation, and perhaps through a new (non-intimate) relationship with your ex-partner. I think that Linda will reach a stage of forgiveness, because even at this early stage she feels a certain sadness for Stephen. I feel that, somehow, she sees the lost vulnerable child in this very abusive person, and in the midst of her own pain finds space to feel sad for him.

> I am also a believer in my faith and I strive to do right by people, and even though I may have slipped on some occasions with him, over time I have found it has dissolved, I have no urge to get back with him. He's in a big enough mess with his life due to himself, without me adding to it. And as much as he has done to us I still wish that he may have some sort of a good life without all the anger and rage. To be honest I feel sorry for him sometimes, because if he could just see all the hurt he causes from what he does, he might see things differently.

One of the principal aspects preventing rehabilitation, and possibly forgiveness, is the presence of rage and anger. This anger is justified and must be vented, but, for the sake of our mental health, we must eventually let it go. Some of the techniques mentioned might help, but developing self-empathy is probably one of the best ways of dissipating it. If you can bring acceptance and compassion to your anger, and experience the hurt that lies behind it, you will promote healing. You went into this abusive relationship with the best of intentions. You tried to make it work, and now you have to feel compassion for yourself, the innocent one who made a bad decision.

The medieval Afghan poet Rumi was a wise individual, and in his poem *The Guesthouse* lies a healing, if difficult, philosophy.

> This being human is a guesthouse.
> Every morning a new arrival.
> A joy, a depression, a meanness,
> Some momentary awareness comes
> As an unexpected visitor.
> Welcome and entertain them all!
> Even if they're a crowd of sorrows,
> Who violently sweep your house
> empty of its furniture.
> Still, treat each guest honourably.
> He may be clearing you out
> For some new delight.
> The dark thought, the shame, the malice,
> Meet them at the door laughing
> And invite them in.
> Be grateful for whoever comes,
> Because each has been sent
> As a guide from beyond.

Chapter 12

If You Have an Abusive Personality, Can You Change?

This cancer eats my soul,
Even as I grow older.
I have not the gift of wisdom,
It is not possible.
I can give good advice,
I can see the problems,
I can offer solutions,
I am intelligent,
But my soul is contaminated,
The generosity of my spirit stifled in the stench of hatred.
Self-hatred.
From the cradle, I have carried this seed.
Forever blooming.
Manured by the fear of abandonment.
Never feeling good enough.
Soured by perfectionism.
Even as I grow older.
I cannot soothe the raging child,
And spray my shame even on those who love me.
Is this always to be?

Jim O'Shea

Despite conducting a deliberate campaign of hurt and control, those of you with abusive tendencies are likely to be shocked if you are labelled an abuser. The first step in any decision to change is awareness, and that label must be applied to you without reservation, to begin the process of bringing about that awareness. As an abuser, you have a strong sense of denial, and you bury deep in your subconscious any recognition of your abusiveness. This is a defence against the pain of the vulnerable, hurt child within you, so you will experience anxiety and fear as your awareness dawns if you contemplate facing the roots of your abusiveness.

You have a choice. You can carry this cancer into old age where it will eat at you until you die, or you can break the pattern that has spread possibly through generations in your family. Unless you decide to do something about it, future generations will be infected, and many more people hurt. Are you ready to face your abusiveness? Are you ready to be vulnerable? Are you ready to face the long hard road of confronting and controlling this cancer? Are you ready to make the decision that you no longer want to be an abusive person? If you are, you will not only help to heal the hurts you have inflicted on your victims, but your own hurt will be assuaged, and you will break the cycle.

I believe that you cannot do this work on your own. Every country has its own specific organisations dealing with people who abuse. There are many battering programmes in the United States. The National Institute of Justice, which is part of the Department of Justice, is heavily involved in such programmes. It also publishes research on how effective they are. Lundy Bancroft, already mentioned in relation to the abusive personality, has twenty years of experience in devising programmes for men who batter. The fundamental aim of these programmes is to offer support to women and children who are victims of abuse. Bancroft trains professionals on best practice for intervening with male batterers, and becoming involved with the victims of these abusers. Bancroft was also a former co-director of Emerge, the country's first counselling programme for men who batter. Founded in 1977, it is now a leading organisation working to end violence in intimate relationships.

There are three organisations in Ireland providing a service to deal exclusively with abusive men. These are MOVE (Men

Overcoming Violence; www.moveireland.ie), MEND (Men Ending Domestic Violence; mend.ie) and MODV (Men Overcoming Domestic Violence). They are voluntary organisations supported by the Department of Justice, Equality and Law Reform. They work in co-operation with each other, and do not encroach on each other's geographical areas. All three have representatives on the Domestic Violence Intervention Programme. You should find a branch (listed on their websites) within reach of where you live. Their services are free, and their aim is to support the safety of women and children by having what I imagine are very challenging group sessions for abusive men. In these sessions, you will be challenged to take responsibility for your violent behaviour and to change your thinking and behaviour. They also provide specific and effective behavioural programmes to help perpetrators to cease abusing. Their belief is that violence is a learned behaviour. The conclusion would, therefore, be that what is learned can be unlearned.

I could not trace any organisation that deals with abusive females.

Those who work on programmes in Ireland enjoy the satisfaction of seeing some of the abusive participants change for the better and stop abusing. But this work can also be frustrating, and facilitators also experience the disappointment of trying to deal with abusive men, who are not willing to change. Global research reflects this, showing that some programmes are ineffective while others have a positive impact on women's safety by suppressing battering. Their first priority is the safety of women and children. They help batterers be aware of their behaviour, and a batterer can learn in a group setting how abuse hurts their partners and their children. Groups also hold men accountable for their behaviour, and provide a setting for positive change. On the other hand, the abuser is surrounded by violent men, and may not be inclined to reveal the inner pain that often promotes abusive behaviour. Strange as it may seem, there are abusive people who get pleasure and satisfaction for hearing about the sufferings of victims. Such groups do not change the abusive personality type, and some abusers on programmes try to manipulate the facilitators, and 'butter them up'. They also know that the police, if called to a domestic incident, will take a favourable view of the fact that they are attending a programme. But, at the very least, abusers who wish to change learn violence avoidance techniques and are educated on abuse and violent behaviour.

Ultimately, if such programmes are not always successful, it is not because of any lack of dedication by their facilitators, but because of the extreme difficulty perpetrators experience in being vulnerable, and being able to embrace self-change. So it is important that you are motivated by the desire to change, rather than enter any programme because you are coerced by the courts or by the threat of your partner leaving you. I believe that self-motivation is the most important ingredient in ensuring your success on any programme.

Before entering such programmes, it is also important, and required by some groups, to deal elsewhere with the mental health issues that you, as an abusive person, are more than likely to suffer from. People with abusive tendencies often experience mental health issues such as depression, anxiety, suicidal feelings, and addiction. In Ireland, as in other countries, there are some marvellous voluntary organisations offering free help for these. Mental Health Ireland (with at least 104 local mental health associations) has an excellent mental health information service, which you can avail of. On its website (www.mentalhealthireland.ie) you will find, for example, contact information for AWARE, a major organisation with a countrywide network of branches. One of its aims is to educate sufferers about depression. It has a helpline, but its main way of helping depressed people is through confidential support groups. Be aware that confidentiality has limits, which will be explained to you by the facilitators of these groups.

GROW is another worthwhile organisation where you can find support. It is a voluntary movement and does not have waiting lists. It, too, has branches all over Ireland, and, like AWARE, its main activity is the establishment of group meetings where any mental health issues can be explored, and where the interaction of group members is geared towards supporting each member.

The HSE has excellent services to cater for mental health issues. Each HSE area in the country has anger management, anxiety reduction and stress reduction programmes. Your first port of call is your GP, who will assess possible treatment. The GP may refer you to the outpatient clinic that is headed by the local psychiatrist, who heads a multidisciplinary team under the aegis of the HSE. The multidisciplinary teams of these community mental health centres consist of psychiatric nurses, psychologists, social workers, cognitive behavioural therapists and occupational therapists. Some of these may engage other family members if necessary. You may also be referred to a day hospital, which means that you can live at home and be treated. The consultant psychiatrist who sees you at the outpatients' clinic will also be responsible for you in the day hospital. There is also the option of attending a day centre, which is staffed by psychiatric nurses and sometimes occupational therapists.

If you are feeling suicidal, the Samaritans provide a 24-hour listening service. Your GP will also assist you, and may refer you to the appropriate agency that deals with suicide. The National Office for Suicide Prevention (www.nosp.ie) provides a very good information service that will direct you to the appropriate place for help.

I believe that counselling is also an effective way, and possibly the most effective way, to confront abusive behaviour and tendencies. I am convinced that an emotional re-experiencing of the pain of abandonment can largely erase the abusive pathway that was laid down by an insecure attachment. Counselling, therefore, is a place where you can both deal with the mental health issues that plague abusive people and directly confront your abusive behaviours. But I am convinced that unless you really want to change your abusive behaviours, counselling will not work to any significant degree, no more than programmes to deal with abuse. The programmes mentioned above have the advantage of involving other family members, while counselling is largely a solitary affair. However, when the perpetrator has explored the abusive behaviour sufficiently well, other members can become involved in family therapy. I do not believe that couples counselling is effective. Research shows that the abuser becomes defensive when the question of violence is brought up, and generally leaves counselling. He may also try to control the session and use it as an opportunity to further blame the victim. Worse still, the victim's assertions may arouse his anger, and leave her open to even more severe abuse at home, where she is unprotected.

Counselling, of course, is expensive and you may not be able to afford private counselling, but you can avail of free mental health counselling services under the aegis of the HSE, which will also help you deal with any mental health problems. Addiction counselling services are provided through the HSE's network of 32 local health offices. You can contact these addiction services through the link 'Local Health Office' on the HSE website (www.hse.ie). Alcoholics Anonymous are a good source of support for alcohol addiction.

Unfortunately, state mental health services, while comprehensive, have long waiting lists. Psychiatrists are extremely busy, and may not be able to see you sufficiently often, and more psychologists are badly needed. Cutbacks during the recession also make it more difficult for the state body to put fully staffed operating structures into place. Private counselling offers a more regular, albeit expensive, alternative, and offers a way to deal specifically with your abusive behaviour. If you can afford private counselling, inform yourself about the different types of counsellors available before you make a decision. Your doctor will give you a list of local counsellors in your area, and you can talk to some of these on the phone before making up your mind about which one you would like to attend. Mick Cooper, Professor of Counselling at the University of Strathclyde, details counselling theories in his book *Essential Research Findings in Counselling and Psychotherapy: the facts are friendly.* Donald Dutton specifically mentions counselling theories that are especially relevant to abusive personality types. You could also contact any of the umbrella accrediting groups, such as the Irish Association for Counselling and Psychotherapy (IACP), for information about counsellors in your area. The IACP has a very good website (www.irish-counselling.ie).

As a person with abusive tendencies, you will find counselling challenging, but the counsellor will gradually form a good relationship with you, and this allows him to make strong challenges without your becoming intimidated. Because abusive people distrust others, it is likely that you will not trust him, even if you have voluntarily come for counselling. You may use your persuasiveness, logic and charm, and want the counsellor to take you at face value. You may find yourself trying to manipulate the counsellor, and minimise or even deny the abuse, or present yourself as the victim. This is dishonest. It will not gain you anything. It is a waste of money. Trying to shed abusive tendencies requires courage, information and honesty. You must be willing to be vulnerable in revealing shameful aspects of your behaviour. It will be difficult for you to give up control, and to be vulnerable and honest in the presence of a stranger! This, however, is how change is effected.

Beverly Engel, Connie Fourré and Lundy Bancroft outline steps that will help you confront your abusiveness, and I will use my own experience to supplement these. I believe that the first step is to learn about the abusive personality, the characteristics of abusers, and the importance of attachment to the primary caregiver, as outlined in the early chapters of this book. Then you can move to explore childhood with your therapist, and as you progress through therapy, I hope that you will 'touch' your inner abandoned child. I believe that this is the most important work you have to do. If you succeed, you begin to feel sadness for that tiny, wounded child who needed love, and, for whatever reason, did not get it. It began to feel unloved and unlovable, and created the adult enveloped in shame and rage. For people with abusive tendencies it is very difficult to 'touch' that child hidden beneath their frozen feelings. It normally takes a long time, and part of this journey is acknowledging that you have been abused or neglected by your parents, and have learned abusive behaviours from one or both of them. This is difficult to do. You may not want to blame them, or you may not wish to confront the buried feelings of anger towards them that you are now directing at your partner, your children, or other people in your life. But whatever the cause of your abusiveness, you must accept that you are responsible for your abusive actions.

In the safety of your counsellor's room you will be able to confront your abusive parent(s) through talking, child work, artwork, the unsent letter perhaps, or whatever techniques the therapist uses. Part of this will be exploring your anger and rage that has tormented you all your life and fuelled your abusive behaviour. One of the best ways to explore anger is to keep an anger diary, and perhaps bring it to counselling for each session. This will help you identify the triggers that spark the anger. Your counsellor will help you manage the anger, and divert it away from your partner. Abusive people are unable to self-soothe, so I sometimes suggest vigorous techniques such as running, swimming or using a punch bag. These vigorous exercises, however, can sometimes increase the rage, so gentle exercises may be more beneficial for you. These include breathing exercises, stretching and walking, and doing meditations. Your counsellor may direct you to centres that teach techniques on how to manage anxiety and tension, which are part of the abusive personality.

While you are taught to manage your anger, you will continue to probe issues underlying abuse – power and control – so it is vital in individual counselling to explore how you control. To do this, examine closely the daily tactics you have used, and see, for example, if you frequently check to assure yourself that your partner loves you. Perhaps, you often test her to assure yourself that she is yours and yours only. Maybe you insist on affection or sex when your partner doesn't feel like it, or refuses because she is busy with something else, and you get angry and try to make her feel guilty. You might be obsessed about where she is and what she is doing at all times, or convinced that she is cheating on you.

Remember that possessiveness is nourished on feelings of abandonment and feelings of not being good enough. You attach rather than love. Suffocate rather than liberate. Your therapist will help you restructure the internal image you have of yourself, formed at the core when you were an infant and is now outside conscious awareness. Changing your core can take a long time, and involves the counsellor watching the emotions that underlie your urge to control and bring them into awareness. If you are a male abuser, your therapist will put some focus on your father. Donald Dutton found that the biggest contributors to the abusive personality were, in order of importance, 'feeling rejected by one's father, feeling a lack of warmth from one's father, being physically abused by one's father, being verbally abused by one's father, and feeling rejected by one's mother'. As a male, you get much of your identity from your father, and if he only gave you conditional love, and punished you, the results were disastrous for you.

As you slowly and painfully increase your understanding of what makes you abusive and how you control, you can begin your journey of making some amends to your victims. This means taking full responsibility for your abuse. No excuses! No minimisation! It was wrong. It hurt others. It was deliberate. You had an agenda. You were selective in choosing your victims. You could have chosen non-abusive behaviour, irrespective of how your brain was programmed during early childhood. I know that you are beset by toxic shame, but being ashamed of hurting others is good shame. Feel it. Acknowledge the hurt unambiguously, and apologise. Make a written and verbal apology. This apology must be sincere, accepting full responsibility, promising never to repeat the abusive behaviour, and pledging to take steps to eradicate it. It will take a long time before you fully realise how destructive abuse is, so try to put yourself in the victim's shoes, and imagine what it must have been like for him or her. This will be difficult for you, because abusive people lack empathy. One of the best ways to understand the hurt is to get the victims to write a detailed account of your abusive behaviour, and how it affected them. I believe that the emotional impact of this on you will be greatly increased if you read these written statements to your counsellor. That takes great courage.

Writing an account of their suffering will also be healing for the victims, but it will also arouse their righteous anger, which they may verbally direct at you. It is important for their healing and for your own that you do not become defensive. This will not be easy for you, because you were accustomed to vent your anger on them. Now you are the vulnerable one. But if you do not give them space to show their hostile feelings, their suffering will be increased.

It is extremely helpful to enlist the help of other key people, such as close friends. This makes it more likely that the abuse will never commence again, because it involves admitting your abusive past. Again, this is difficult for people with abusive tendencies, who hide their hurt and shame behind bravado and narcissism, and see vulnerability as weakness.

If you have the courage to take this path, you will gradually begin to respect your partner and recognise her/his boundaries. I suggest that you learn about boundaries, and this will help you see that healthy relationships show parity and respect in every aspect of being together running a house and rearing children, having equal responsibility, sharing, communicating, mutual handling of money, listening without interrupting, and giving space for your partner to be angry. Think boundaries! Become acutely aware when you are tempted to breach them. Be aware of the triggers and false beliefs that kick into action at that time. Pay attention to how your abusive tendencies are ignited if you feel ignored, insulted, rejected or shamed.

As I mentioned earlier, about 45% of abusive relationships are bilateral, or mutually abusive. One of you may ultimately feel that you cannot go on living like this, and perhaps begin the process of trying to change the abusive relationship. This is a major task, and it is unlikely that you would be able to do it on your own. A counsellor would be vital to help you find your way through a process of changing your relationship to a non-abusive one. Beverly Engel offers a way of doing this, which would involve a great deal of communication on your part. This will not come easy, because abusive people do not listen, and always want their own way. And there are two of you with similar tendencies, so the counsellor is vital in teaching you how to listen and communicate. You will have to decide if your relationship can be saved, and agree to stop abusing each other. It involves both of you committing to change, and exploring the past with open minds. You will have to commit to stop blaming each other for relationship difficulties and to be willing to change the abusive dynamics of the relationship.

If you can agree on this, you can share your life stories and begin to understand the influences that bred the abusiveness, such as childhood neglect, abandonment and abuse, as outlined in this book. Allow time for each of you to tell your story without interruption, and you can begin wherever you wish. You should also look at the interaction between your parents, as well as how they treated you. Was there an abusive atmosphere in the house with much blaming, fighting, shouting, or long silences? As you later discuss each story see how it affects you, and see if you have any empathy for each other. This is probably unlikely at this stage, because feelings do not suddenly become unfrozen.

When you have told and discussed your stories, you should begin the healing process, as discussed above. This means sitting down and acknowledging and taking responsibility for your part in the abusive relationship. Listen to each other's unconditional admission without interruption and without becoming defensive. Both of you might also write down how you were abused, and how you abused. Take plenty of time to ensure as much detail as possible. Then apologise for each abusive incident noted, and agree to move on.

Moving on means discussing how you each niggle and annoy each other by pressing the other's buttons to stoke anger, rage, shame or guilt, all ancient experiences coming from childhood. This discussion is very important because it increases your understanding of your partner and helps to avoid further conflict and abuse. It will be difficult for both of you to draw up boundaries, because these are alien to abusive people. But you can take practical steps to concretise them by writing down your partner's behaviours that are particularly annoying and objectionable to you. These would include anything from the list of abusive behaviours already explored in earlier chapters. Discuss these, and pledge to avoid them in future. This is not a perfect world, and humans are imperfect, so you will find that you will have to compromise on some issues.

Some therapists and researchers state, and I agree, that the success rate of changing the abusive outlook is low, partly because the abuser must make the most honest and strenuous efforts to overcome this behaviour. They may not be ready to change, because not everyone is able to bear the pain of exploring the root causes of why he or she has become an abuser. Neither are many able to bear the shame of revealing this dire trait to another. Beverly Engel is more optimistic, but I feel that overcoming abusiveness is a lifelong task. You will abate your anger and your shame. You will succeed in largely rewiring your brain, and become calm and kind. But, in addition to the above steps, you both may have to go for individual counselling to get at the roots of the abuse.

I believe, however, that the urge to control never leaves, and so you can become a calm and happy controller. Therefore, to prevent this, you must always be keenly aware of your need to control. When you have completed therapy, your ways of controlling can become more subtle. You will know that control is the basis of abuse, and still not be aware that you are in the controlling mode. Indeed, you may learn many psychological methods of controlling from your counselling. Knowledge breeds power, and power breeds control. I am convinced, however, that having gone through counselling, and always being on the alert for controlling your partner, or your children, you will succeed in creating a non-abusive relationship. I suggest that you ask your partner or your children to help you, and challenge you if they suspect control. I am certain that your shame and rage will abate and your self-esteem will grow after such considerable effort.

Your final and very difficult task will be to forgive yourself. This is vital if you are to move on and establish loving relationships. But even recognising that you need self-forgiveness is a sign that you are now cognitively and emotionally aware of your history of abuse and the damage it has caused. I think that the aid of an empathic counsellor will be necessary to help you forgive yourself. At that stage, you will indeed have lopped the heads off that many-headed monster – abuse.

Afterword

I hope that this book has given you a better understanding of abuse. It is an emotionally difficult behaviour to explore. Some of this behaviour is ghastly, and has a devastating impact on victims. Nonetheless, however difficult an abusive situation seems to be, however despairing your frame of mind, even if the obstacles seem insurmountable you do not have to remain in an abusive relationship. There is always hope, always a brighter future. In that context, I will leave you with what Linda thought were her final words, before her husband returned from Canada and threw her into turmoil.

> It's hard to explain, but I can now see every side of a problem for people. I like to listen to them when they have worries, or are upset. I try to help them when they ask for advice based on what I have learned from my story. I always try to help them see that it's not going to be all doom and gloom, and that there is always a way forward. It may not be easy, and it may take time, but there is always a solution and a way forward.
>
> I have also started to be grateful for what I have. I have a beautiful son, who brings me joy each day of my life. I enjoy the lovely sunny days when we can play football or go for a walk. I enjoy the simpler things in life. Material things don't mean all they used to mean to me anymore. I believe from my experience I have gained knowledge that I can apply to myself, but also that I can help friends and family. I am also trying to learn currently how to take it 'one day at a time', and to stop worrying about the

future. I still do this sometimes, but I am now aware of doing it, and, therefore, I can try to control it and try to live and enjoy the present!

They say that we learn from our challenges and mishaps in life. In my case, I believe this to be true. I learned that things happen in life that you cannot do anything about; things you may not want happening in your life, but you have no choice. I also have learned to open myself up to people and how differently they may live their life, or what they believe.

What I would say to anyone who is going through, or has gone through, a story similar to mine is not to be afraid to leave if you need to. You only get one chance in this life, and you have to live your life and be happy. You have to move on and learn from the past, and hope for the future. Live in the present and deal with each challenge as it comes. Bit by bit, day by day, a new life will be growing all around you, until one day you stand back and say, 'I did it, and I am so happy with my life that is now peaceful'.

These were Linda's words, before her world was shattered by the return of her husband from Canada. Her emotional chaos on his return does not take from them. They are, however, the words of someone who thought she had completed her grieving. But look at her final words, when she had at last emotionally shaken off the shackles of abuse and completed her grieving. Note how emphatic and confident she is. She has finally abandoned the rosy picture of the charming Jekyll, and clearly sees the ugly Hyde. Thankfully, Linda completed her grieving in about four weeks of counselling and processing. I expect that you will find comfort and hope, when you read the relief, freedom and clarity in her final statement.

What I can look back and say now, is that Stephen did me a big favour. I am glad he came back, because it opened up all my wounds and heartache and made me deal with it all again, so that I am finally over it.

Stephen, of course, went from his caring side to the ugly selfish side in a short period. He turned cold once things weren't going his way with his plans for us. He reduced his contact with Jack, and generally went back to the man that I know he is – a self-consumed, abusive man. I am glad, though, that this also happened. I went from the confused, painful stage to clarity very quickly, because I now have knowledge of how the abuser works and the cycles they go through. I knew this would happen. I knew that the nice Stephen wouldn't stay too long. He was never there to begin with, but when my head was overruled by my feelings and emotions I placed him on a pedestal, and couldn't see beyond the good times.

I can see clearly beyond the good times now. I see him for exactly what he is. To type those words and say them after these years of hurt is such a FREEDOM to me. I CAN SEE HIM FOR EXACTLY WHAT HE IS. I ACCEPT WHAT HE IS, AND I LIVE MY LIFE. I am finally FREE. I am free in my mind now. I may have been free physically for a long time, but in my mind I wasn't. I now look at him and feel pity, and also a sense that our lives are so different, and that we are such different people. I have no idea how we ever got on, or had anything in common. He is completely different to me in every way.

I don't have feelings of anger, sorrow, longing or love. I see him on the days he visits my son. We are civil to each other. There's nothing else. Sometimes it just feels like a business transaction. I'm here for my son to get a chance to know his father. I am here for my son because I love him deeply and care for him deeply. Otherwise, I wouldn't be in his company for anything, as I have no need or want to be in it.

I can now meet him, and he has no hold on me at all. At the end of visiting time, I get into my car and happily say, 'let's get back to our life'. I no longer find him physically attractive. He is no longer this big strong man that would take care of us and love us. He is a mere lost boy in my eyes these days. One that doesn't know where he is going or what he wants and, unfortunately, will probably cause havoc to someone else.

And as my story ends, I love to wake up to every morning, and experience FREEDOM and PEACE – my mind and heart are freed at last – and now I can move on in my life with NO EMOTIONAL BAGGAGE holding me back! Take the power you have within you and claim YOUR FREEDOM!

Bibliography

Abbey, A., Zawacki, T., Buck, P.O., Clinton, A.M. and McAuslan, P. 'Alcohol and Sexual Assault', *Alcohol Health and Research World*, vol. 25, no. 1, 2001, pp. 43–51

Ackerman, R. *Silent Sons: A Book for Men from Troubled Backgrounds and Those Who Love Them* (London: Thorsons, 1994)

Adapt Services, *Lean On Me: An Information Guide for Women Living with Domestic Abuse* (Dublin: Adapt Services, 2001)

Alison, J. and McGonigle, C. *Liberating Losses: When Death Brings Relief* (Cambridge, MA: Perseus Publishing, 2003)

Aposhian, M.A. and Cooper, A. *Sex, Lies & Honesty: Signs of Sexual Acting Out And Some Ways to Heal the Hustle Inside You* (Online article, 1998)

Arehart-Treichel, J. 'Parent's Verbal Abuse Leaves Long-Term Legacy', *Psychiatric News*, vol. 4, no. 13, 2006, p. 28

Bancroft, L. *Why Does He Do That? Inside the Minds of Angry and Controlling Men* (New York: Penguin, 2002)

Baron-Cohen, S. (ed.), *The Maladapted Mind: Classic Readings in Evolutionary Psychopathology* (Hove: Psychology Press, 1997)

Baumhoefner, A. *Financial Abuse of the Deaf and Hard of Hearing Exposed* (Edina, MN: Beaver's Pond Press, 2006)

Beattie, M. *Codependent No More: How to Stop Controlling Others and Start Caring for Yourself*, 2nd edition (Center City, MN: Hazelden, 1992)

Bagley, C. and D'Augelli, A. 'Suicidal Behaviour in Gay, Lesbian and Bisexual Youth', *British Medical Journal*, no. 320, 2000, pp. 1617–18

Belenky, M.F., McVicker Clinchy, B., Goldberger, N.R. and Tarule, J.M. *Women's Ways of Knowing: The Development of Self, Voice, and Mind*, 2nd edition (New York: Basicbooks, 1997)

Bowlby J. *Attachment and Loss: Separation, Anger and Anxiety* (London: Random House, 1998)

Brackenridge, C. and Fasting, K. *Sexual Harassment and Abuse in Sport: The Research Context* (Online article, 2002)

Bradshaw, J. *Healing the Shame that Binds You* (Deerfield Beach, FL: Health Communications, 1988)

Byrne, T., Maguire, K. and Byrne, B. *Bullying in the Workplace, Home and School: Questions and Answers* (Dublin: Blackhall Publishing, 2004)

California Attorney General's Office, *The Financial Abuse of Seniors* (2007)

Capacchione, L. *Recovery of Your Inner Child* (New York: Simon & Schuster/Fireside, 1991)

CARI, *Annual Report, 2008/9* (Dublin: CARI Foundation, 2009)

Center for Sex Offender Management, 'Female Sex Offenders', a project of the Office of Justice programs (US Department of Justice, 2007)

Clarke, N. *MEND (Men Ending Domestic Abuse) Report. Referring Men: An Exploration of Frontline Workers' Needs for Referring Abusive Men to MEND Domestic Abuse Intervention Programmes* (Waterford: The Men's Development Network, 2010)

Cloud, H. and Townsend, J. *Boundaries: When to Say Yes and How to Say No to Take Control of Your Life* (Michigan: Zondervan, 1992)

Commission of Investigation, *Report into the Catholic Archdiocese of Dublin* (2009).

Coonan, R. 'Breaking the Last Taboo: Child Sexual Abuse by Female Perpetrators', *Australian Social Work Journal*, vol. 30, no. 2, 1995

Cooper, M. *Essential Research Findings in Counselling and Psychotherapy: The Facts are Friendly* (London: Sage Publications, 2008)

Corby, B. *Child Abuse: Towards a Knowledge Base*, 3rd edition (Maidenhead: Open University Press, 2009)

Corry, M. and Tubridy, Á. *Depression: An Emotion, Not a Disease* (Cork: Mercier Press, 2005)

Cosc, *National Strategy on Domestic, Sexual and Gender-Based Violence, 2010–2014* (Dublin: The Stationery Office, 2010)

Davis, G. *A Report of 2007 Domestic Violence-Related Fatalities in Lucas County, Ohio* (Toledo, OH: University of Toledo, 2009)

Debbonaire, T., Debbonaire, E. and Walton, K. *Evaluation of Work with Domestic Abusers in Ireland* (Bristol: Online book, 2004)

Denise, C. *A Mother's Tongue: Overcoming Verbal Abuse* (Clermont: FL: Jawbone Publishing, 2004)

Dutton, D.G. *The Abusive Personality: Violence and Control in Intimate Relationships*, 2nd edition (New York: The Guilford Press, 2007)

Dutton, D.G., Nicholls, T.L. and Spidel, A. 'Female Perpetrators of Intimate Abuse' (Online article, n.d.)

Dutton, D.G. and Nicholls, T.L. 'The Gender Paradigm in Domestic Violence Research and Theory: Part 1 – The Conflict of Theory and Data', *Aggression and Violent Behaviour*, no. 10, 2005, pp. 680–714

Eardly, J. *Bullying and Stress in the Workplace: Employers and Employees – A Guide* (Dublin: First Law Limited, 2008)

Engel, B. *The Emotionally Abusive Relationship* (Hoboken, NJ: John Wiley & Sons, 2002)

Evans, P. *The Verbally Abusive Relationship: How to Recognize it and How to Respond*, 2nd edition (Avon, MA: Adams Media Corporation, 1996)

Evans, P. *Verbal Abuse: Survivors Speak Out on Relationship and Recovery* (Avon, MA: Adams Media Corporation, 1993)

Ferrara, F.F. *Childhood Sexual Abuse: Developmental Effects Across the Lifespan* (Pacific Grove, CA: Brooks/Cole, 2002)

Fiebert, M.S. *References Examining Assaults by Women on Their Spouses or Male Partners: An Annotated Bibliography* (California State University, online publication, 2009)

Foa, E.B., Keane, T.M. and Friedman M.J. (eds), *Effective Treatments for PTSD* (New York: The Guilford Press, 2000)

Forward, S. *Toxic Parents: Overcoming Their Hurtful Legacy and Reclaiming Your Life* (New York: Bantam Books, 1990)

Fourré, C. *Finding Your Way Through Domestic Abuse: A Guide to Physical, Emotional, and Spiritual Healing* (Notre Dame, IN: Ave Maria Press, 2001)

Friday, N. *Jealousy* (Glasgow: Fontana/Collins, 1989)

Gilbert, P. *Depression: The Evolution of Powerlessness* (New York: The Guilford Press, 1992)

Gleeson, B. *Changing Minds, Changing Practices* (Kildare County Council, n.d.)

Goodman, L., Fels, K. and Glenn, C. *No Safe Place: Sexual Assault in the Lives of Homeless Women* (National Online Resource Center on Violence Against Women, 2006)

Graham-Kevan, N. *Domestic Violence: Research and Implications for Batterer Programmes in Europe* (Article sent to author by Nicola Graham-Kevan, 2007).

Graham-Kevan, N. 'The Psychology of Women's Partner Violence: Characteristics and Cautions', *Journal of Aggression, Maltreatment & Trauma*, no. 18, 2009, pp. 587–603

Groth, A.N., Hobson, W.F. and Gary, T. *The Child Molesters: Clinical Observations* (Online book, 1985)

Hardiman, M. *Healing Life's Hurts* (Dublin: Gill & Macmillan, 1997)

Hardin. K. and Hall, M. *Queer Blues: The Lesbian & Gay Guide to Overcoming Depression* (Oakland, CA: New Harbinger Publications, 2001)

Harthill, S. 'Bullying in the Workplace: Lessons from the United Kingdom', *Minnesota Journal of International Law*, vol. 17, no. 2, 2008, pp. 247–302

Harvey, J.H. and Miller, E.D. (eds), *Loss and Trauma: General and Close Relationship Perspectives* (Philadelphia: Brunner-Routledge, 2000)

Hegstrom, P. *Angry Men and the Women Who Love Them: Breaking the Cycle of Physical and Emotional Abuse* (Kansas City: Beacon Hill Press, 2004)

Herman, J.L. *Trauma and Recovery: From Domestic Abuse to Political Terror* London: Pandora, 2001)

Hester, M. *Who Does What to Whom? Gender and Domestic Violence Perpetrators* (Bristol: University of Bristol in association with the Northern Rock Foundation, 2009)

Hill, M., Stafford, A. and Green Lister, P. *International Perspectives on Child Protection: Report of a Seminar, 20 March 2002* (University of Glasgow, 2002)

Hines, D.A. and Malley-Morrison, K. 'Psychological Effects of Partner Abuse Against Men: A Neglected Research Area', *Psychology of Men & Masculinity*, vol. 2, no. 2, 2001, pp. 75–85

Hopper, J. *Child Abuse: Statistics, Research, and Resources* (Online article, 2009)

Hopper, J. *Sexual Abuse of Males: Prevalence, Possible Lasting Effects, and Resources* (Online article, 2009)

Horgan, J., Muhlau, P., McCormack, P. and Roder, A. *Attitudes to Domestic Abuse in Ireland: Report of a Survey on Perceptions and Beliefs of Domestic Abuse Among the General Population of Ireland* (Dublin: The Stationery Office (Cosc), 2008)

Horley, S. *Power and Control: Why Charming Men Can Make Dangerous Lovers* (London: Vermilion, 2000)

Health Service Executive, *Open Your Eyes: Elder Abuse Service Developments* (Dublin: Health Service Executive, 2008).

Health Service Executive, *HSE Policy on Domestic, Sexual and Gender-Based Violence* (Dublin: National Communications Unit, 2010)

Hunter, M. *Abused Boys: The Neglected Victims of Sexual Abuse* (Lexington, MA: Lexington Books, 1990)

Itson, C. *Adult Cyberbullying: The Anonymous Attacks of Adult Cyberbullying Cross the Line and Enter the 'Real World'* (Online article, n.d.)

Jantz, G.L. and McMurray A. *Healing the Scars of Emotional Abuse* (Grand Rapids, ML: Revell, 2009)

Jones, A. *Next Time She'll Be Dead: Battering and How to Stop It* (Boston: Beacon Press, 1994)

King, M., Semlyen, J., Tais S.S. et al., 'A Systematic Review of Mental Disorder, Suicide, and Deliberate Self-Harm in Lesbian, Gay and Bisexual People', *BMC Psychiatry*, no. 18, 2008, p. 70

King, M., Smith, G. and Bartlett, A. 'Treatments of Homosexuality in Britain Since the 1950s: An Oral History – The Experience of Professionals', *British Medical Journal*, no. 328, 2004, p. 429 et seq.

Kohut, M.R. *The Complete Guide to Understanding, Controlling, and Stopping Bullies & Bullying at Work: A Guide for Managers, Supervisors, and Employees* (Ocala, FL: Atlantic Publishing Group, 2008)

Lerner, H.G. *The Dance of Anger: A Woman's Guide to Changing the Pattern of Intimate Relationships* (London: Pandora, 1989)

Levenkron, S. *Cutting: Understanding and Overcoming Self-Mutilation* (New York: W.W. Norton & Co., 1998)

Lew, M. *Victims No Longer: The Classic Guide for Men Recovering from Sexual Child Abuse*, 2nd edition (New York: Quill, 2004)

Lipshires, L. 'Female Perpetration of Child Sexual Abuse: An Overview of the Problem', *Moving Forward Newsjournal*, vol. 2, no.6, 1994

Long, M. *Ma, He Sold Me for a Few Cigarettes* (Edinburgh: Mainstream Publishing, 2008)

Longueepee, R. 'Systems of Control: The Global Legacy of Institutional Child Abuse' (Reach Canada: Equality and Justice for People with Disabilities, online article n.d.)

McGee, H., Garavan, R., de Barra, M., Byrne, J. and Conroy, R. *The SAVI Report: Sexual Abuse and Violence in Ireland* (Dublin: The Liffey Press in association with Dublin Rape Crisis Centre, 2002)

McGee, H. et al., *SAVI and SAVI Revisited: Long-Term Effects of Disclosure of Sexual Abuse in a Confidential Research Interview* (Dublin: Rape Crisis Centre, 2005)

McKay, S. *Sophia's Story* (Dublin: Gill & Macmillan, 1998)

Mamen, M. *The Pampered Child Syndrome: How to Recognise it, How to Manage it, and How to Avoid it* (London: Jessica Kingsley Publishers, 2006)

MEND (Men Ending Domestic Abuse), *How to Deal with Domestic Abuse: A Self-Help Book for Men who Want to Change* (Waterford: MEND, n.d.)

Miller A. *The Drama of Being a Child: The Search for the True Self* (London: Virago Press, 2002)

Miller A. *For Your Own Good: Hidden Cruelty in Child-Rearing and the Roots of Violence* (London: Virago Press, 1999)

Munro, K. 'Male Sexual Abuse Victims of Female Perpetrators: Society's Betrayal of Boys' (Online article, 2002)

NiCarthy, G. and Hutt, J. *Getting Free: A Handbook for Women in Abusive Situations* (London: The Journeyman Press, 1991)

Ó Flaithearta, L. *Dúil* (Baile Átha Cliath: Caoimhín Ó Marcaigh, 1953)

Ombudsman for Children, *An Investigation into the Implementation of 'Children First: National Guidelines for the Protection and Welfare of Children'* (Dublin: Office of the Ombudsman for Children, 2010).

O'Moore, M. 'A Guiding Framework for Policy Approaches to School Bullying and Violence' (Dublin: Trinity College, n.d.)

Osborn, S.T., Kosman, K.L. and Gorden, J. *Wounded by Words: Healing the Invisible Scars of Emotional Abuse* (Birmingham, AL: New Hope Publishers, 2008)

O'Shea, J. *When a Child Dies: Footsteps of a Grieving Family* (Dublin: Veritas Publications, 2008)

Parkes, C.M. *Bereavement: Studies of Grief in Adult Life* (London: Penguin Books, 1998)

Rivers, I. 'Long-Term Consequences of Bullying', in C. Neal and D. Davies (eds), *Issues in Therapy with Lesbian, Gay, Bisexual and Transgender Clients* (Berskshire: Open University Press, 2000), pp.146–59

Roberts, D. and Roberts, D. *Another Chance To Be Real: Attachment and*

Object Relations Treatment of Borderline Personality Disorder (Lanham, MD: Jason Aronson, 2007)

Roubicek, J. *Financial Abuse of the Elderly: A Detective's Case Files of Exploitation Crimes* (New York: Ruby House Pub, 2008)

Sanderson, C. *Counselling Survivors of Domestic Abuse* (London and Philadelphia: Jessica Kinglesy Publishers, 2008)

Schiraldi, G.R. *The Post-Traumatic Stress Disorder Sourcebook: A Guide to Healing, Recovery, and Growth* (Los Angeles: Lowell House, 2000)

Schore, A.N. 'Attachment and the Regulation of the Right Brain', *Attachment and Human Development*, vol. 2, no. 1, 2000, pp. 23–47

Schore A.N. 'The Effects of a Secure Attachment Relationship on Right Brain Development Affect Regulation and Infant Mental Health', *Infant Mental Health Journal*, no. 22, 2001, pp. 7–66

Schutte, B. *Fixing the Fighting: A Guide to Using Mediation in Settling Disputes and Resolving Conflict in the Workplace* (Cork: Oak Tree Press, 2003)

Smith, J. 'Male Circumcision and the Rights of the Child' (Online article, n.d.)

Stephenson, K. 'Cutting and Self-Injury Common Behaviour Among Teens' (Online article, 2009)

Stevens, J. 'Men and Physical Abuse by Women' (Online article, n.d.)

Stevens, J. 'The Problem of Physical Abuse in Pregnancy' (Online article, n.d.).

Vardigan, B. 'Verbal Abuse of Children', *Consumer Health Interactive*, 2009

Wang, C.-T. and Holton, J. 'Total Estimated Cost of Child Abuse and Neglect in the United States: Economic Impact Study' (Chicago: Prevent Child Abuse America, 2007)

Weiss, E. *Surviving Domestic Violence: Voices of Women Who Broke Free* (Sandy, UT: Agreka Books, 2000)

Whitfield, C.L. *Boundaries and Relationships: Knowing, Protecting and Enjoying the Self* (Deerfield Beach, FL: Health Communications, 1993)

Will, N. *Within the Walls of Silence* (Bloomington, IN: Xlibris Book Publishing Co., 2000)

Women's Aid, *Annual Statistics Report 2007* (Dublin: Women's Aid)

Worden, W.J. *Grief Counselling and Grief Therapy: A Handbook for the Mental Health Practitioner*, 3rd edition (New York: Brunner-Routledge, 2003)

Index